HOW TO LOSE YOUR MIND IN NO TIME

A guide to a more aware and joyful life, starting from wherever you happen to be

Hanaan Rosenthal

TMI Publishing
Providence, RI

Look for
"How to Lose Your Mind in No Time"
on Facebook

Twitter: @BarefootHanaan

Too Much Information Publishing

61 Doyle Avenue

Providence, RI 02906

www.tmipublishing.com
Cover art by Regina Wamba

ISBN: 978-1-938371-01-1

Bookstore shelving information

SEL021000 SELF-HELP / Motivational & Inspirational

SEL016000 SELF-HELP / Personal Growth / Happiness

SEL032000 SELF-HELP / Spiritual

Contents

Foreword

You are the creator of your own experience. You have defined the life you live, and you continue to create the life you choose.

This is a very old idea, isn't it? Think about it—virtually every major wisdom tradition—including religions which center on a belief in God, teach us to understand and work from this idea. Yet for so many of us, we struggle with this truth. We deny it, we embrace it in thought but not in action, we forget it, we judge ourselves as being "bad at it". We don't embrace it.

In this book, Hanaan Rosenthal offers a perspective on why this may be the case for so many of us, and what we can do about it. In this, too, there is nothing new. The book next to this one on the shelf in the bookstore probably dealt with some of the same ideas. So why is this one different? It is different because Hanaan is not a self-help guru, a yogi, or a psychologist. He's someone who has discovered something remarkable for himself -something about the full power of creative agency we all possess but rarely bring into flower—and decided to figure out how it works and share it with us.

When I was first getting to know Hanaan, I was fascinated by how he seemed to do so many things well, and struck by his creative energy. He always seemed to be trying to create something new, was always involved in a new venture. Yet he never seemed anxious or restless. Quite the contrary—he acted as though the things he sought to bring into being would simply come into being by and by.

One day, while visiting at his house, we discussed the idea of the role of self perception in weight loss. Our beliefs, he explained, generated both dispositions and actions, and the energy we thus put out into our world yielded experiential returns which suited them. Believe it, in other words, and you will make it true. These were not new ideas, we both agreed, but they made sense. Yet, I told him, they seem so difficult to enact. People could know about how beliefs and habits of mind work, they could understand their ego, their subconscious mind, and so on—but something made actual transformation next to impossible for most of us.

Hanaan disagreed. "It's simple," he contended, "It's not next to impossible; that's a limiting belief. It's a process, it takes time, but it's simple to do".

Over the years that followed, I learned more closely what Hanaan meant: I watched him transform himself through the simple processes he shares in this book. He went from being a slightly overweight, fairly ordinary looking guy into a vegan who runs half marathons barefoot, and doing it without ever going on a diet or following a workout schedule. I watched him grow more prosperous, even as our economy sputtered. Regardless of the situation, he seemed happier and more at ease with himself and with others. Nothing seemed to bother him.

Not that this was a straightforward process for him, as you'll find out. Like all of us, it took a long time for the relationships between Hanaan's protective ego and his limitless subconscious to form, and (like all of us) his ego's foundation goes deep and his thought processes continue to follow old, long established pathways—responding to his emotions, placing obstacles in his path, rambling on autopilot. But Hanaan has learned how to observe these interactions and, with steady practice, strategically alter them in ways that leave him feeling happy and healthy.

One day, Hanaan told me he was working on this book. He'd been living the experience of consciously creating his reality, and he figured that while a lot of books were out there which touched on many of the principles which informed his own growth, he felt that his own process had taught him a lot about what happens when we attempt to enact those principles—especially those things which often function to inhibit our process. Sharing these ideas and experiences with others, he thought, would be great fun.

He nailed it.

Hanaan isn't a therapist or a physicist. He's a guy who lives in a Victorian tenement building in Providence with a lovely, wild garden in the back. He has a wife who's out of his league and two young children who are already smarter than him. He writes computer programs for a living, is a reluctant sports fan, loves Dylan, plays scrabble, has a good sense of humor (as you will learn) and is a good photographer.

He's content with his life, and he simply wants to talk you through how you can become content as well.

Enjoy this book.

David Hayes,

Director

Academic Enhancement Center

University of Rhode Island

Preface

About five years ago, while on a twelve-hour flight to Israel with my family, I was passing the time reading a book suggested by my mom. She often gives me books to read, and, being a typical son, I usually casually flip through them before tossing them aside. This one was different. The book was Joe Vitale's *The Attractor Factor.* The subject matter and new perspective it revealed were exhilarating. It was as if a door had opened and I walked through. What I found was a premise, alien at first glance, but on a deep level, it felt like home. My intuition that there were simple explanations to complicated problems and that people held amazing power to shape their lives was mirrored in the text. I felt that an old part of me, which I had long ago forgotten, had been awakened, never to sleep again.

Given my fascination with explaining complicated matters in simple terms, my natural angle was to take all that information and make it accessible to everyone.

Pieces of this book have rattled in my mind for a few years. I wrote and published a massive Mac programming book some years ago, so I knew I had the perseverance to pour about a hundred thousand words into a Word document in a reasonably well-conceived pattern. In fact, in the past three years, I've written the first and second versions of this very book. Both were scrapped before anyone else read them.

For about a year thereafter, I kept thinking that I *should try* to write the book again. I decided that when the book was ready to be written, it would just be written. I stopped trying.

This publication is the result. While it was me writing the book at no-one's request, I was not in charge and did not control the process. I just saw my fingers move and hoped to keep up. All I could do was picture it on a bookshelf; I visualized myself opening the box from the publisher and how much fun that would be.

WHY CHANGE?

When contemplating life changes, the first question that came up was simply, *what is the point?* Why would I get up one day in the middle of a comfortable life and want to change anything? I was married to a woman I loved, had two amazing kids, was happily self-employed, and generally had a great life. What could be better?

The answer I arrived at was one I would like to share with you: your life doesn't have to be awful for you to want it to be better.

Actually, you don't have to want to change anything in particular—certainly nothing material or concrete. I am still happily married. My kids are older but still amazing. I still live in the same house and work for myself. What changed for me was internal. It was my awareness.

No matter what your state of awareness is, there's always ample space for personal growth. You can have a good life and still decide to increase your awareness; of course, it can also be that you live a rather confused life and feel rotten much of the time. In that case, you may truly desire change.

Whatever your starting point is, you can live a deeper, fuller, and more joyful life. Even if you love your life exactly as it is right now, you can always discover amazing things that can add substance and depth to your experiences.

Much like bungee jumping, it is sometimes easier to propel yourself to new heights if you first experience a deep fall. The world is full of stories about people who came through pain and made amazing things happen. But we can't live someone else's life or wait for a tragedy to give us a new perspective and shift our priorities. Life, experience, and state of mind are the starting points from which we all move forward in this journey.

The subject of making changes to our physical forms, our relationships, and our financial situations has been studied and discussed ad nauseam. Strike a conversation with anyone on the street, and soon you'll learn what he or she would change in their lives if they could. Most of us often wave the "this is how I'd prefer my life to be" banner. This book deals with how to bring about change. However, it also discusses *change* as an umbrella subject rather than focusing on altering specific aspects of your life. I believe that any changes we make in life involve the same process, whether in finance, love, fitness, or health. Similar methods and ways of thinking can change any aspect of life.

I find that I'm much more likely to change my habits when I understand why I am taking certain steps. Logical explanations always seem to come, in my experience, at a time when I am ready to allow change to happen.

You may find some suggestions harder to accept than others, but overall I hope you will find this book a reasonable step in your journey toward change.

ACKNOWLEDGMENTS

Thank you to my parents, who once I stopped avoiding at eighteen, hating at twenty, rejecting at twenty-two, and finally forgiving at twenty-five, have become amazing, supportive and positive presence in my life.

To Johanne, Olivia, and Aylam, who suffered through the full range of unedited and unabridged emotions, theories, and opinions I ran through (and still am) in pursuit of this text.

To my many writing spots around Providence: Wild Flour Vegan Bakery, University Heights Whole Foods Market, Seven Arrow Herb Farm, Seven Star Bakery, Blue State Coffee, Lazergate, Garden Grille, Amtrak Regional on the North East corridor, and various sofas around the house.

To the many teachers who inspired me along the way: Eckhart Tolle, Joe Vitale, John Asaraf, Dr. Wayne Dyer, Bruce Lipton, Esther Hicks, and many others.

CHAPTER 1

The Meaning of Life

What is the meaning of life? This question has been the subject of philosophical debate and a Monty Python movie, but not much else. After all, why ponder something with so little practical merit? But what if, like many unanswerable questions asked throughout time, the answer is so simple that we have all just overlooked it? The answer I can give you, in the form of the rest of this book, is based on my observations of my greatest passion: people.

To answer the eternal question above, to the extent that I am able, I would say that *the meaning of life and the secret to our existence is simply how we feel*. Think about it. When you're feeling bad, your life stinks; when you feel good, everything else is good.

Life is a collection of shared and personal experiences. We live life through our experiences, and everything we experience is filtered through how we feel. Feeling makes up the quality of existence. The same is true for how an individual feels in a shared experience. A person's existence is only ever experienced through his or her individual mind. It cannot be any other way.

Life is a collection of experiences, shared and personal. How you feel, or how each individual feels in a shared experience is what makes up the quality of our existence.

So what's more important than you, me, and all our fellow humans feeling good? I can't think of anything

However, how we feel is much more than the result of random events in our lives. How we feel is the reason things happen in our lives the way they do.

Of course, simple answers to basic problems are often complicated to implement. Simply understanding that feeling good is "where it's at" may be only the first step toward getting there, but it is an important step.

In this book, we will venture into the muddy waters of what to do to shift your life toward a more joyful state.

If the meaning of life is indeed how we feel, then what's more important than to focus on feeling good?

WHY PEOPLE SUCCEED

Actions aren't the reason a person succeeds in a specific aspect of life. The person's state of mind causes the success. In other words, actions matter, but actions come as a result of thoughts and beliefs. Since the subconscious controls most actions, *trying* to act like successful people act can only have temporary results at best. After some time, you will revert to the pattern of following your own beliefs and habitual ways of thinking.

This book is not going to show you what happy, successful people do. Instead, it is going to show you how they think, and how you can train your mind to think like them. Since *doing* comes out of believing, once you change what you believe, your actions are naturally going to follow.

There are many books written by successful people who share what they did to achieve success: how they started a career, what organization tools they used, how they managed their time, how they ate less, how they had sex with more or less frequency, and other such tidbits. These elements about someone's life may be fascinating, but we have to realize that they cannot be duplicated to achieve similar results in your life. Something in their mental makeup and core belief generate situations that are in line with their *wants*. They have the ability to see things how they want them to unfold, and they naturally have very few mental blockers. What they do is not the cause of their success; rather, it is the means to their success. What they do is the result of how they think.

If you're looking for something beyond what you have now, maybe it's time to put away old conventions and look at life from a different perspective.

CHAPTER 2

A Good Life

A good life. Isn't that what it is all about? Having a good life transcends occupation, gender, age, geographical location, or financial situation. Having a good life is a self-describing state. It's a state of mind rather than a result of having a lot of money or any other material condition. Even if it may seem that material possessions are why life is good, identifying possessions as the cause of a good life is a very common misconception. In addition, having a good life has its own scale. Only the individual can know whether he or she has a good life.

If this book were dedicated to one goal, it would be you having a good life. If you could do that, if you could somehow flip a switch and make it happen for yourself, would anything else really matter? Everything that's important to you would fall into place. Anything that currently seems like an insurmountable problem would be worked out, and the impossible would seem easy to solve.

But what makes a good life? How can we break it down into components so that we can analyze it, reverse-engineer it, and build it for ourselves? Let's try to pick apart what we call life so we can see what might make it good.

FUTURE, PAST, AND PRESENT

Throughout our lives, our thoughts are divided among three focus points: what happened in the past, what will happen in the future, and what is happening right now (the present). For the most part, we are occupied with the past and the future and pay very little attention to the present. Let's take a closer look, primarily at the past and future, and see what we spend so much energy on.

The past is not reality. It is not even real—it is only a subjective, fragmented memory of events you have observed. Our point of view as humans is narrow, and our accounts of the past are painted with our beliefs to such a degree that it can be more accurately described as imagination than what actually happened.

And what about the future? The future is nothing but a mind trick. We don't know what will be in the future, and the range of possibilities is vast. Pondering the future can be a powerful tool of creation, but for most people it is a habitual source of anxiety, fear, and eventual pain.

Our lives happen now, in the present. You've probably heard that enough times to find it annoying. Even when we think about the past or the future, we are not in the past or future. We are thinking about them in the present. This is not psychological or philosophical; it is common sense. If I put a cardboard box in my living room and paint it like a castle, I can sit in it and imagine I am in a castle, but I am still in my living room in my house. Pondering the past or future has a place and a purpose, and there's nothing inherently good or bad about it. In fact, this act of pondering is happening right now.

Is now good? If life happens now (in the present), the question of whether one's life is good can be also phrased this way: *Is my now good?* Whether the now (or present) is good is a result of a single factor: how you feel. Feel good and your present is good. When your present is good, life is good.

Let's make a distinction between two different types of *feeling good*. We start by asking if there's a bad good. There is a harmful feel-good that does not fit into this formula. You can imagine that the good you feel after a good workout is not exactly the same as the good you feel after lighting a cigarette, eating twelve cookies, or enjoying whatever you consider your substance of choice.

The result of the first feel-good is that it brings on wanting to do more things that feel good, and the activity itself can have other benefits, such as a healthier life, happier relationships, etc. The other feel-good has a negative opposite that eventually hits us hard.

Let's look at eating cookies as a simple example. This has nothing to do with overeating or control; this is just an illustration. Who doesn't love to eat cookies? They are just too good to resist! So there you are, and there's a plate of cookies on the table. Eating one or two cookies can make you happy, but will eating more make you happier? Well, theoretically, yes, so you eat three more. You start to feel the sugar rush and a bit of heartburn. The pain is starting to catch up, but it will clear out in an hour. At this point, the cost is about even with the benefit. You feel equally as bad as you feel good. Eat one or two more cookies and you start feeling guilty and out of control. Now the bad/negative feeling slightly outweighs the good/positive feeling. Finish the whole plate, and the ten minutes of sweet taste in your mouth might be offset by a couple of days grappling with the reality that you are overweight, ashamed of your eating habits, have a stomach ache, etc.

At some point, the scale tipped, and the cookies went from being a small pleasure to an emotional liability. So, there's a type of feeling good that results in more feeling good and a type of feeling good that results in feeling bad.

LIFE CONSISTS OF MANY NOWS

Since our *now* can be sometimes good and sometimes bad, and our lives are made of many *nows*, how good our lives are can be determined by asking ourselves the following question: putting all the now moments of the day, week, or month together, are there more good feelings than bad feelings, and by what margin? What margin would you like? Do you even care?

Our lives are made of moments, and how we feel in each moment can help us determine whether it was a good moment. The more good-feeling moments in our lives, the better our lives are and the longer we want to have a better life.

This book is not about how to make more money, find a spouse, get a better job, eat better, or even know how to meditate or do yoga (which I can't seem to be able to do). It is about how to feel good more of the time.

Sure, all these things may be components of feeling good, and in your journey to feeling good, you will certainly encounter more positive experiences in these areas. Truly feeling good transcends all these aspects of life. In a way, feeling good starts with feeling good. Aspects of feeling good, such as eating right and not smoking, are a result of the steps we take to feel good and not the other way around.

MORE ABOUT FEELING GOOD

There's a long-standing, widely held belief that feeling good is always associated with feeling bad. There are two sides to everything in life, and anything good has an end, followed by misery. Love has hate, peace has war, serenity has turmoil, etc. This is somewhat true, but it is hardly the entire story.

Everything good in the material world, as Tolle states beautifully in *The Power of Now*, has the bad already built into it. For example, if you bought a new car and identified it with having a perfect car, it already has the bad feeling built into it, since the car will certainly get scratched and an equal amount of bad feeling will surface when it does.

We may believe that feelings are a result of events; however, the trigger for how we feel is much more complicated. Unless we break the cycle of how we were programmed to feel, we will go back to feeling the way we're programmed to feel one way or another.

There's another aspect to feeling good that has no negative opposite. This is the joy of simply being alive. Regardless of your financial, social, marital, or professional status, you can feel good simply because you are a part of this amazing life we all share. In fact, the degree to which your worldly status is positive is a result of how good you feel—not the other way around.

IS IT FAIR TO FEEL GOOD?

Feeling good can sometimes feel like a luxury that we can only partake in after we resolve all the problems in the universe. Can I feel good as long as someone else is oppressed, hungry, hurt, abused, mistreated, bombarded, trapped, unemployed, enslaved, neglected, molested, sickened, or otherwise experiencing negative things? Feeling good while those things are going on in the world can feel horribly selfish instead. While it may sound like an argument that comes from a compassionate place, we need to give the idea that we can't be happy while others suffer a closer look.

If we waited for everything to be right in the world before allowing ourselves to be happy, we would never even get the chance to be happy. Are you more able to help others when you reflect misery or when you emit happiness? Right. You can be happy and still be loving, compassionate, and helpful toward people in need. In fact, being happy positively influences everyone around you, and being depressed will have the opposite effect.

It is not fair to feel happy. If we want to help others, if we want to make this a better place for all to live in, and if we want to instantly help our friends, family, and anyone we encounter have a better life, it is our duty to figure out how to be happy. Your obligation is to have a good life. Get to it—it's not that difficult and can be a lot of fun!

CHAPTER 3

Core Beliefs and Reality

For the most part, we see life as a random array of events. Somewhere, we believe that life is the fortunate or unfortunate result of that endless and chaotic array of events. Things happen *to* us, and we do the best with the circumstances. We try to make lemonade when we're handed lemons, and when that doesn't work, we can unload a well-worn set of complaints to a sympathetic ear.

We might believe that our happiness is nice when it *happens*, but it's of no real consequence. We may not view our own happiness as a goal all by itself.

LEVELS OF REALITY

While reality appears to be one flat layer of things that happen, it is actually composed of multiple layers—each layer adding its own influence for how things manifest in our lives. The most basic, overruling reality is that of the universe. It is responsible for us having basic beliefs, such as that we can't fly and the knowledge that we can't be underwater for too long. Additionally, there's the reality of the world, which we also share with other humans. We also have a reality for our country, state, city, neighborhood, and family. Each layer has common beliefs that affect all members of that layer. For example, at the family level, all members of a family may believe that Bob, the maternal great-grandfather, was the best author in the country. The rest of us may not even know who Bob is, so he's not at all a part of our reality, but he is a part of every member of that specific family's reality.

While we share these layers with others, our personal realties affect our own lives the most. Our personal realities are vastly different from the realities of other people. Reality is based on our observations of the world around us and is subject to our deeply rooted beliefs, prejudices, and points of view.

It is common knowledge that the *way we see things* impacts our lives. But *the way we see things* is not simply an aspect of our reality. The way we see things *is* our reality. Everything that happens revolves around our perceptions. Our point of view may be the result of our reality, but more important, point of view and point of focus create our reality in the first place and give it depth, flavor, and meaning as we go through life. Without perception, there is only empty space, energy, atoms, and photons. Let's take a closer look at this idea.

HOW WE OBSERVE REALITY

A common belief is that we all swim in one big container of reality, seeing it from slightly different angles. This view of life needs rethinking.

Reality is so intertwined with belief that we see things differently from other people—even people we live and work with. After all, the lens through which we see the world is extremely narrow and covered with heavy filters. We see what we are used to seeing and what we believe there is to see. Most important, however, what we see constitutes a tiny fraction of what there is to see. While the subconscious is privy to millions of pieces of information, the conscious mind, through which we experience life and build a theory of what reality is, can only handle a handful of information. The subconscious filters a huge portion of reality and shows us a small, carefully selected collection of details that fit our understanding of the world and match our existing beliefs.

We discard things that fall outside of what we believe. Our reality, therefore, consists only of what the subconscious allows us to see. Blind spots are a good example of this phenomenon. For example, a blind spot is an obvious personality trait we see in other people that they don't seem to see themselves.

The fun thing about blind spots is that if they exist so obviously in other people, we have to imagine that they also exist in you! We have a whole set of behaviors that we are completely unaware of, but all our friends are very much aware of these behaviors. If this doesn't make you cry, it *has* to make you smile. Blind spots are habitual actions that the subconscious takes on our behalf, but it prefers to hide them from us. Since we're not present while they are manifested, they are not a part of our reality. They are hidden because if we saw ourselves do these things, we probably would want to stop. For example, it is possible that you are not nice to people during a blind spot, or maybe you overeat, smoke, or engage in some other form of self-abuse. The subconscious gets to manipulate your relationships and health and leaves your conscious mind with a completely different impression of "who you are."

To sum up, there's a huge difference between my reality, your reality, and the reality of every other person. There is no separation between reality and we viewed it. There is no other reality beyond that which we perceive, and changing how we perceive reality can be a vehicle for dramatic change.

ARE EVENTS IN YOUR LIFE RANDOM?

The idea of reality being *created* can be a bit baffling. Isn't reality simply a result of everything that is going on? And even if creating reality is somehow possible, there are so many variables—how can someone or something be actually planning reality out and creating it? Reality, from the human viewpoint, appears to be random and chaotic.

Well, it is anything but. The events in our reality can appear random simply because we tend to be inside of them. Seeing the events as they happen is like walking in a corn maze without a map, trying to make up the pattern of the maze. If we chart our moods, actions, and events in our lives, a clear pattern will emerge—a pattern that will be very similar to our reality.

To better understand events in our reality and how they shape our lives, try this simple exercise: pick up a daily or Sunday newspaper and find a color photo. Now look at that photo through a magnifying glass. All you can see are random color dots and shapes. Imagine that you were tiny and living down there among the dots. Now imagine that someone told you that the dots create a clear picture when you are above them. Since you can only see a handful of dots at a time, that would surely surprise you. Now, imagine that you wanted to annoy that person who told you about the pattern, so you took paint and changed a good number of the dots. However, to your dismay, the big picture hardly changed. In order to make the picture unrecognizable you would have to change at least half the dots, if not more.

There's also another reason why we miss the pattern created by our life events, actions, moods, and behaviors. This reason is closely related to a strong defense mechanism humans have: we naturally reject the notion that we are responsible for things that happen in our lives. It is much more comfortable for us to think that life is random rather than to accept that we create the reality we live in.

In some very real way, we are responsible for our life situation. Whom we do (or don't) live with, our health, our occupation, the money we have or don't have, and virtually everything else that makes up our reality is a reflection of our overall state of mind. Understanding and slowly accepting that part of us plans and executes our reality is essential if we want to make any significant, lasting changes.

Okay, stop reading now for a second and listen. I need your undivided attention for this. Now let me repeat: the idea that we somehow create our own reality can be foreign and possibly even a bit scary. If you seem to be uncomfortable with that idea, know that you are not rejecting it. Your ego is. It is your job to find, somewhere in your mind, a place where this theory sounds somewhat acceptable.

Then of course, you may be completely happy and comfortable accepting responsibility. If so, you're well on your way, but there's still much to be done.

THE WANTER IS NOT THE CREATOR

So, if we are responsible for our situations, why is it different from how we wish it to be? If I created my reality, you say, it would surely be different in many ways. I would make my boss really hot and easygoing and relocate my office to a beach front property. Why, then, is there such a gap between how I want my life to be and how I create my life?

The answer is simple. Our life situation is a reflection of our whole selves and are not formed based on what we want. We may think we want things such as love, money, a nice place to live, and a nice place to work. But deep inside, we may have strong resistance to those very same things.

We have to realize that there is much more to us than the parts we are aware of. Deposits of anger, shame, insecurity, and other trolls could be hanging in there from our past, tainting our self-perceptions and contributing to the process of shaping our realities. The sum of all those deeply rooted beliefs act as a blueprint for our lives.

WHO MAKES IT SO?

The reflection of the whole of you, the seen and the unseen, is the blueprint for your reality. And when there's a blueprint, there's a builder, which is the entity that takes the plans and turns them into your life. This would be your ever-powerful subconscious.

The subconscious has the ability to see everything that's going on, and it is in charge of our lives somewhere between 95 percent and 99 percent of the time (Biology of Belief, Bruce Lipton). It is also about a million times more powerful than our conscious minds, processing information and making things happen (or un-happen) without our conscious minds even knowing what goes on.

The subconscious is responsible, via a myriad of means, for everything we have and don't have in our lives. It regulates our jobs, love lives, social scenes, health, weight, money, houses—everything.

Besides making material things pop in and out of our lives and changing our situation, the subconscious has another supremely important job: it regulates how we feel.

It is common to believe that life is made of an infinite number of factors and events. We observe everything somewhat objectively and react with our actions and feelings. How we feel and react is a reasonable result of the random things that happen to us.

This might have made sense except we're aware of only a minuscule fraction of everything going on around us. The bits that make our reality have been carefully picked with the purpose of showing us what we are used to and what we feel comfortable with.

Perhaps mood is the biggest telltale to the constantly repeating pattern in life. If life were random and life events were responsible for how we felt, then our moods would have no discernible pattern. We would be happy for a week because good things happen, be upset for a day, feel nothing special for a couple of months, and then feel really depressed for a few days. This isn't the way mood works. If you charted how you felt every hour for a month, you would see a clear pattern. Your subconscious is working hard to maintain that mood pattern, and your ego is working to keep that pattern hidden from you. Recognizing that mood pattern and being okay with the idea that your subconscious regulates your mood takes courage and is an important step in making your life more of what you want it to be.

WHY IT IS HARD TO BELIEVE

Grasping the idea that we somehow create our own reality is not easy. The subconscious creates our reality, and the protective layer called the ego is between our subconscious and conscious selves. The ego is like our very own press secretary. You say, "Can it be that a part of me makes my life what it is?" And your ego jumps in and answers, "What? Nonsense. Life is random! Think about all the negative things in your life. Do you really want to believe you create those? Do you really want to go there?" Mostly, you prefer not to.

To better understand where the rejection of the self-creation idea comes from, we have to understand the perceived threat it represents to the ego. One of the most important jobs the ego has is to keep us safe, and the safest thing the subconscious knows is just that: what it already knows. Any suggestion that things are not as we understand them can be difficult to integrate. In this case, there's an additional danger: awareness. The ego rules by telling us that we are separate from all that is, and the idea that we are becoming aware is a threat.

At first, the ego simply tries to have us ignore any signs that such a theory even exists. Remember, the subconscious is responsible for what we do and don't notice, so when the idea of self-creation comes up, it is disregarded for the most part.

When this idea is presented to you directly and you have to respond, your subconscious simply disregards it as crazy or not scientifically sound. Most people you know would probably laugh if you told them that they, in various ways, are responsible for their own life situation. This makes it easy to brush aside the idea as new age, guilt-inducing, pointless baloney.

Having said all that, I want your full attention for the following sentence. I need you to hinge anything and everything that is not right in your life on these words: the important events in your life are not random. Important, landmark events in your reality are planned out by a variety of means, including your own subconscious.

These events form a pattern that repeats and makes our lives what they are. This pattern is a direct reflection of the whole you, which includes the parts you know, and more important, includes the parts you don't know. This key point can be summed up in a mathematical equation:

Your life/reality = the little you know about yourself + a whole bunch you don't know about yourself.

This can also be flipped around to give you a glimpse at what you are unaware of in yourself:

What you don't know about yourself = your life/reality - what you know about yourself.

Since many things you believe about yourself may be false or exaggerated, the things you're unaware of can be even more shocking and hard to believe or accept.

It is not necessary to understand where your issues come from to remove them from the creation process. All you'll have to do is reinvent yourself. It is very possible, although it can be a somewhat elusive process.

The idea of self-creation may come off as completely illogical. We have to consider that our logic does not come from some universally true set of facts. It comes from our current understanding of the world and how things are. If this understanding is flawed, the logic we use to decide what is a solid theory and what is nonsense will also be flawed.

If you reject the idea that you are in some pivotal way responsible for your reality yet don't like your reality and look for how and why it is not optimal, this may be the first "weird" idea you adopt that will start some positive change in your life.

THE BLAME FACTOR

The concept of blame is another reason the idea of you as the creator of your life can be difficult to grasp. Blaming anyone else for how your life is can only lead to more frustration. Sure, your parents may have really done a job on you, your spouse may be less than perfect, and your dead-end job, which is complete with an oppressive, out-of-control boss, can be hard to get away from. But any effect those factors have on your life is only as great as you allow it to be. This allowance has been developed over years, so it may seem as if there's no way that something in you made it happen. Until now, you may not have known that you had a part in it, and it may take some time to settle. But regardless, certain people are a part of our lives because we allowed them to be. They are there to fulfill a function that matches a need we have. This need is most likely buried somewhere in you.

The other end of blame is our need not to be at fault. A typical defensive statement is, "It is not my fault that (fill in the blanks)." Right, it is not your fault—but if it is a negative aspect of your life, it is up to you to clean it up.

We can easily live our lives looking for someone to blame, but when we're ready to change so that we feel good more of the time, we have to do away with blaming. This goes both ways: blaming others for anything we don't like in our lives and defending ourselves from blame. Blame is a blocking agent for change.

MANIFESTATION IS EASY TO DISREGARD

The self-creation aspect of life is easy to overlook. For the most part, we keep on creating reality the same way. We also believe that reality is what it is, due to our observation of reality. Hence, our belief of reality is constantly confirmed.

Since the creation of life is based on our belief about how life is, we then observe our situations and see that, indeed, reality is as we thought it was. We believe that the world is as we see it. This puts us in a cycle where we create our lives in the same format we always had and at the same time have no reason to believe that life can be any other way. The part where we create our own reality may be most foreign to us.

Other than that, it all sounds just right: I observe the world (life, reality, etc.) as it is, and I believe that the world is as I see it.

Our part as the creator is the most important ingredient in this equation, but it is easy and comfortable to miss.

CHAPTER 4

How You Create Your Life

Understanding how the subconscious orchestrates our lives and the mechanism that makes our lives is important in order to change things in a meaningful way. The first and most important thing to understand about life, reality, and the current state is that it is constantly happening. Let's look at *how* it is happening.

THE BLUEPRINT

Anything that is created has a plan, and any event in our lives is an accessory to that plan. While there are random events that have no bearing on our situations, the collective pattern of meaningful events make it what it is. This pattern is based on a specific blueprint.

That blueprint is the whole of you.

It's easy to say, "I have so much good in me and my life sucks. How can I possibly be the creator of my life? If I were indeed the creator, I would be rich and retired in a villa in Mexico with my beautiful significant other." The missing piece in this scenario is that the blueprint is not just the parts of you that you are aware of. It is the entire package. The parts that you are unaware of are greater than the parts you know. The subconscious, including its connection to the world, other people, and the sediment of past events in your life, is what makes up your existing beliefs. These beliefs paint every aspect of your reality. In fact, if you wrote all the things that are not right in your life, you will come very close to describing the parts of you that you are not aware of.

Changing that blueprint is very difficult and very easy at the same time. Imagine holding a hammer and a knife and having to break a piece of glass and cut a piece of cloth. When you apply the right tool to the right task, it can be very easy. However, when you try to cut the glass with the knife and break the cloth with the hammer, you are in for a long and frustrating time. Finding how to manipulate the pieces of the conscious and subconscious minds can be difficult, take a long time, and generally drive us nuts, but once we understand certain things, change is not that difficult.

THE ONGOING CREATION PROCESS

It's easy to look at events in our early life and see their effects on us. It is also easy to believe that, since those things happened so long ago and still affect us so profoundly, they will take a long time to resolve. We believe that reducing the influence our childhood has on our lives today must involve digging deep down to the place where those early, painful events are stored. After all, they are the cause of the problems we have.

To understand why this is not true, we have to understand the ongoing nature of life creation. Let's paint a scenario that can help with that.

Imagine that you bought a house, and a month after moving in, the neighbor's kid threw a baseball through the window and smashed it. It was a mess. You cleaned it up, but the window was still broken. Since it was the neighbor's kid, you asked him to pay for it or have it replaced. For some reason, the neighbor didn't do so, which left you frustrated. And why shouldn't you be frustrated? After all, your window was perfect until his kid broke the window.

Now it is twenty years later, and the window is still broken. By now, most of the house has been restored three times, has been painted, and has had a new roof put on it. You also take all the windows out for cleaning every year; however, this window was never replaced.

You can say that this window is broken because of the neighbor's kid, and you will be right. This kid now has his own house and his own kids and has long forgotten about that day—you are the one keeping it alive. You are the one refusing to fix the window. The window becomes broken again every time you look at it and do not decide to replace it. Your frustration is the reason for your reaction today. It is not from someone else's actions long time ago.

Our lives are created much the same way. The events that shaped us happened long ago and are mostly forgotten. The personality traits, anxieties, frustrations, eating habits, substance abuse, depression, and other aspects of our lives are still there because we recreate them repeatedly. We don't replace those aspects with positive things. We let the blueprint stand. That blueprint that was created long ago is still the plan used today to recreate your life.

Our role in designing our reality is multifaceted, but here's one where you can see the process clearly. Listen to yourself tell stories and reiterate reality as you see it. Are you full of gratitude about what you have? Are you full of positive, confident dreams about a bright future? Usually not. For the most part, you're focused on something that's wrong in your life. It is completely natural to believe that to change things, you have to focus on what you want to change or what you don't like. But that is not the way it works when it comes to changing your reality. In fact, it is the other way around.

When we create reality, we get more of what we focus on. You tell a story about how unhealthy you are and how depressing it is that you can't be as active as you used to be—and bam! Another reinforcement to your subconscious grand plan. You tell a friend about how difficult it is to find a job, and your subconscious hears that it is hard to find a job as a fact. Is it hard to find a job? Yes, if you believe it is. You just wrote it into your plan.

Almost everything in our lives is up for change. Think about it. Every seven years, every cell in our bodies is replaced! Every day, tens of billions of cells die and regenerate. These come from our faces, internal organs, skin, and hair. Not many things in life stay the same. Money? You make money and spend it all the time. Change is not the issue since the matter of our realities are constantly being circulated. It is just that it's being replaced, piece-by-piece, with the same stuff.

THE STUFF OF THE BLUEPRINT

When assessing the success or failure of any project, there must be some method of measuring success and some units to use for gauging progress.

We may measure our lives by the love we get from friends and family, the money we have in our bank accounts, our positions at work, or maybe by assessing our health and fitness. The subconscious, however, has a more specific measure. When looking at our blueprint and tweaking our lives, it attempts to match how we feel. The subconscious manipulates our lives to the best of its ability to put us in situations where we feel a certain way.

The subconscious has a daily plan for varying levels of love, anxiety, stress, relief, fear, shame, and power. It will literally create and seek situations that will, at different times, induce a specific sensation the grand plan indicates.

The way we feel after a specific event is not a response to a random event, but rather the result of a well-planned and executed scene driven by our eventual emotional reactions.

Not every event in our lives is planned that way, only the ones needed to complete the pattern. If you are accustomed to getting your afternoon shot of anxiety, and it's already getting to be evening, you had better believe that your subconscious will make something happen. Before you know it, you will be comfortably stewing in some anxiety-filled drama as your fix is delivered. But after it has hit its target on an emotional level, things may happen around you that you might not even notice.

THE TARGET IS HOW YOU FEEL

As we saw above, how we feel is not a result, it is the target. In fact, how we feel, or the average feeling we have during the day, is the reason for most of the meaningful events in our lives.

How we feel is the flavor of life. Much like eating at a fine restaurant—the flavor and smells you experience are the grand purpose of the meal. Otherwise, we'd stay at home with a bag of bread and some peanut butter and have the time of our lives. The way it works with food, as you know, is that the chef masterfully plans and prepares every bit of that meal so that it is experienced in that specific order and timing. Similarly, we go to restaurants where we can experience flavors similar to the ones we are used to and have had specific experiences with.

The same thing happens with how we feel. The subconscious is a personal chef; it plans and executes events in our lives to bring in feelings we're used to. Of the many events happening around us, it points out few and urges us to feel and react a certain way.

This does sound like a self-centered way to look at things. "Me, me, me—I am the center of the universe and how I feel is most important." Well, no matter how you look at it, the subconscious is putting our lives together for us, and for the subconscious, getting us to feel a certain way is the most important goal.

BLUEPRINT DETAILS

Our blueprints are quite complicated, as our core beliefs are, so the plan we present for the subconscious to follow may have different levels of feel-good and feel-bad in different parts of our lives.

For example, you may find it easy to have a person to share your life with, love that person, and have an amazing relationship with him/her. However, financially, you may fall flat on your face. On the contrary, you can have the ability to attract money like a flower can attract a bee but have such horrible social skills that people prefer to stay away from you.

Personally, I never had a problem approaching girls I liked and striking up a conversation with them, but since I grew up in a Kibbutz in Israel where money was scarce and having lots of money was a not considered a good thing, I found it difficult to make money. I was sure that money was for other people.

This ability of different people to attract different things dispels the idea that things are innately difficult to get. When you ask a self-made millionaire if making money is difficult, they will laugh. Everything they do makes them money. Money sticks to them wherever they move.

So is it easy to make money? If you ask most people, they will point to having to "work hard," " riding out the bad economy," or other common core beliefs that go around like the flu. But why is it easy for some people? Doesn't it mean that it is difficult for those who believe it is difficult? That is exactly what it means.

And as always, the circular feedback system is working: when we believe that it's difficult to make money, it is reflected in our reality. We can observe our reality and see that indeed, we were right, making money is difficult. And on and on.

The many facets to our personalities will make it easy to test some of the methods we will look at later on. Instead of having to face a plate full of things to change, we can start with one small thing and go from there. For now, change will have to wait. We have more to cover first.

THE MASTER BUILDER AND THE ARCHITECT

The blueprint for our lives has something to do with our deep-seated beliefs. Who is then responsible for taking that blueprint and making it into reality, and what is our part in it?

The master builder is the subconscious. It is a million times more capable than the conscious mind. It can move mountains, start and dissolve grand enterprises, woo anyone at any time, and fulfill anything written in the blueprint. The subconscious is unstoppable, but can only act within the parameters of the plan.

Even though it is powerful, the subconscious is missing something critical, the essential seed of any creation process, imagination. The subconscious can't break new ground. It can't change your plan, add to it, or decide that some of it is just too difficult. In fact, your subconscious acts as if your blueprint is so perfect, that if you try to change it, it will throw everything at you but the kitchen sink, trying to stop you from straying from your plan. The subconscious likes things just the way they are.

If you are overweight, who is responsible for you remaining overweight to that exact same level year after year? That is a lot of work, you know! If you always lack money, imagine how hard your subconscious is working to maintain your life just on the brink of being able to pay the bills. You think you are the hero that makes the rent payment at the eleventh hour every month? Think again. You are the one that unknowingly signs off on the plans to make this happen the same way, again and again.

I realize you are taking a little beating here, but this information is not exactly material they taught you in school. Most people like to complain about their lives; they like to point out what's wrong. They have no idea that these very actions are responsible for you getting more of exactly what you are complaining about.

But all this has a good side as well. First, though, we have to look beyond the possible conclusion that anything negative in our lives is our fault. We have to let go of the concept of fault because it's not helpful and blocks efforts to make positive change. It's pointless.

Instead, I'll offer you another way to look at it: if your life getting better were indeed someone else's responsibility, you would have absolutely no chance. However, now that you know that the power is all yours, maybe, just maybe you can do something about it.

Remember that the creation process can't be started or stopped because it is in perpetual motion. Since reality is constantly being created, the choice is between being a conscious part of the process or a passive bystander. You can imagine which option can bring on more pleasant results. While we can and have unknowingly created some things we're not happy with, the same level of energy can be used to create exactly what we want.

That's because even with all the power the subconscious has, it still follows our commands. It does that methodically and without ever looking back. If your subconscious is an army with ten thousand soldiers, then you are Alexander the Great. It is your inspiration and your ability to project how you want to feel. It's your innate ability to imagine how you want your life to be and charge it with positive emotion. All those abilities are what make you the amazing creator and powerful reality-bender that you are. Your capacity to design your own reality is going to amaze you.

GOODNESS FROM THE UNIVERSE

Money doesn't grow on trees, but it grows much like trees grow. The universe we are lucky to be a part of is always expanding. Look at what was an empty lot a year ago—it is now full of plants growing through the cracks, or a building is popping up in it. Look at a meadow that was freshly mowed last month. It is now full of flowers, plants, and weeds. Each one started from a seed and is now making its own seeds, attracting bugs and other animals.

Expansion and proliferation is everywhere, not because people are trying harder but because this is the nature of the universe. The same power that makes a seed grow into a tree can get you anything and everything you want. It may be hard to believe all that, but I urge you to consider it as a possibility.

CHAPTER 5

Ways of the Ego and Subconscious

The subconscious has many ways of making sure we don't stray too far from "home base." The comfort zone is one of its most well-known methods. The way our comfort zones work is very simple. When we stray out of our comfort zones, we start to feel, well, uncomfortable. This sense of discomfort will prevent us from doing stupid things that can hurt us. For example, standing on a flat roof and getting too close to the edge will give you an uncomfortable feeling. This feeling is very similar to the feeling you get in other, less dangerous situations, such as going on the dance floor, talking to someone you're romantically interested in, or whatever makes you uncomfortable.

KEEPING YOU IN CHECK

Comfort zones are used to make sure we don't get too much ahead of ourselves and to make sure we're safe. Let's say that you haven't been promoted in a long time, but being promoted in your field means that you have to network. Unfortunately, you're very shy, so doing what it takes to succeed makes you uncomfortable. This shyness is simply being uncomfortable talking to people, and the subconscious prompts it. Your subconscious could be keeping you safe from becoming too successful or from something it has learned can hurt you. Possibly, in some period in your past, you were hurt in such a way that made you fearful about expressing yourself. Your subconscious has developed shyness to protect you from being in that same situation again. Now, of course, you intellectually know that talking to people has no danger associated with it, but the subconscious was never told that explicitly. Until this issue is handled, you will always be "protected" from the danger of talking to people you don't know.

The subconscious uses self-talk to keep you in line. Statements such as "this will never work" or "it's too dangerous" are negative self-talk. Negative self-talk is your subconscious prompting you to stop whatever it is you were planning to do, and in turn, avoiding harm.

CORRECTIONS

Mostly, the subconscious has a rather easy time avoiding the spotlight. It leads us to believe that this is just how things are. Sometimes, however, unplanned or unexpected events in life change our life situation beyond our comfort zones. For example, you could be awarded a job interview that would give you a higher salary than you ever believed you would could make or scored a date with a girl or guy you believed was out of your league.

In those cases, the subconscious has to take more substantial action to bring you back to your comfort zone. The result is what we know as self-sabotage. An example of self-sabotage is when the subconscious makes us mess up. We fall asleep right before a date starts and miss it, we mention something we shouldn't in a job interview, or we make a stupid purchasing decision that in turn causes us to be late with the rent. Need more examples? Ask around—we all have stories about how we messed something up for ourselves, often with serious life consequences.

Yes, they are responsible for these actions, but they were powerless to prevent them. Once the subconscious is on a course to make something happen or mess something up, it will get its way no matter how much we try, kick, and scream.

CONTROL

Perhaps the biggest trick the subconscious is playing on us is the illusion of control. Understanding that and coming to terms with our general inability as humans to control most of what we do, think, or say will make it much easier for us to make meaningful changes in our lives.

This means, for example, that if you have a problem controlling what you eat, you actually have a different problem. Why? Because no matter what you do, you may be able to control what you eat for a short amount of time, but unless change happens in your beliefs and thoughts, your subconscious will "course-correct" and the weight will come right back. The same applies to money, relationships, social ability, career, and anything else you can think of.

THE SOURCE OF EVERYTHING WE DO

Anything in life involves talking, walking, or using our bodies in some way. The spark for most of those things is a thought. For the most part, actions either start in our heads or go through them.

Now consider this: *you are not the source of most thoughts and actions*. Your subconscious is. Remember that the subconscious is responsible for controlling and managing 95 to 99 percent of our daily activities. This is not at all a bad thing. Every decision we make requires so much data to process that it would be virtually impossible to make a single decision without it. We would not be able to put together more than a few sentences during the day or walk more than a few steps. The simple task of walking or driving would be a terrifying, treacherous activity.

The subconscious achieves this control in various ways. For mundane, everyday tasks such as walking, driving, and talking, it bypasses us entirely and just takes direct control over our bodies.

For other things, it has to be a bit subtler. You see, part of what keeps us going at this point is the illusion that we are in control of our lives, and the subconscious is intent on keeping it this way. It achieves this control by pushing thoughts to our focal points rather than just directly doing it for us.

At any given point, there can be literally billions of possible thoughts that fit the situation we're in. How could we possibly pick from such a large pool of possibilities? We can't. The conscious mind can only have one thought or focus at a time. And since the subconscious is what usually points us to what we end up thinking about, it has a huge influence over our focus, which determines our activities, our moods, and eventually the course of our lives.

Next, the subconscious saturates us with the sense that we are in control and that this particular thought was our idea. It also makes it as clear as possible that this thought represents a real part of our lives rather than the arbitrary scenario that it is. Believing that the thought is reality starts to make the sentiment of the thought into reality. You are the one who identifies with the thought and adopts it as an unquestionable part of your day. After all, if a thought ran through your head, it must be right.

The first step in moving forward is to understand the relationship between you and your subconscious. It is difficult to tweak subconscious thoughts and direct the focus to a more positive direction, and it takes time. Intellectually, it's important to at least understand that the subconscious determines most of your focus.

Let's put this control scenario in perspective. Becoming more conscious or living a more conscious life may eventually mean that we have more say about what is going on, but not in the immediate future. This is not necessarily a bad thing. A way to become more conscious is to observe our lives unfold. We will see that while sitting in the driver's seat, we can still enjoy the view, stop to look at the map once in a while, and carry on a conversation. It is much more fun to observe life as it happens when we realize that somehow, we are not in control, and that it is sort of fun!

You can take this idea for a spin. Next time you're having a conversation (you can start one right now if there's someone in the room), simply observe yourself. You will talk, move, and make facial expressions. Now ask yourself if you have been doing all of that or if it is just happening to you. Am I picking each word and inserting it in the right tone and context? Fluctuating my tone, smiling at the right points, and expressing mood with my eyes? Impossible. Carrying a conversation is far too complex a task for my conscious mind. My subconscious is doing it for me, and pretty well, most of the time. The only time I stall is when I attempt to control what comes out of my mouth and how.

A large part of the work we'll look at in later chapters revolves around the concept of letting go. Relinquishing control. Your life is a cruise, and your role, as the captain, does not require controlling the details but rather setting the course and enjoying the ride. All you need to do is steer occasionally.

THE SOURCE OF A THOUGHT

While we may not contemplate thoughts on a regular basis, they are actually a sophisticated delivery tool for information and ideas. Thoughts are the means by which the subconscious reaches us, the way the ego interrupts us and shares its constant chatter, and the way we receive invaluable messages from the universe.

Let's look at three sources of thoughts: the subconscious, our observer, and the universe.

1. THE SUBCONSCIOUS

Given that the subconscious is responsible for our daily lives and is in control the majority of the time, there's no surprise that it is responsible for the largest share of our thoughts and actions.

Our subconscious constantly directs us to thoughts that align our focus with our beliefs. Those thoughts are intended to keep us on the same path and steer us away from things we're not accustomed to.

For example, if a situation comes up where an external force suggests an activity outside of what is written in the plan, the subconscious makes us feel discomfort. It does this by planting a "don't go there" thought.

A thought is not the only means of subconscious communication. Imagine if, while we drive, the subconscious would make us think through every move. We would have a car crash every minute and take hours getting to the corner store. In most cases, the subconscious simply bypasses the conscious mind and instructs our bodies to take action.

From all the information your subconscious processes through sight, hearing, touching and smelling alone, it only bugs you a tiny fraction of the time. I don't mean two to three percent of the time, but of the billions of details the subconscious is privy to every given moment, you only get interrupted every few minutes, if at all. ("Hey, this house is for sale," or "Hottie at three o'clock!") Your subconscious knows what things you like to pay attention to. It points out those things in the form of a thought, which makes the subconscious conscious.

We cannot control or manipulate thoughts from our subconscious, because by the time we become aware of them, they already happened. There are ways to direct the subconscious to a different set of thoughts, but that will be the subject of future chapters. The only thing we can do with these thoughts is see them for what they are and observe them. All they are is thoughts.

Judgmental and Nonjudgmental Thoughts

Judgment separates the ego (our subconsciously created personality) and our real selves. It's not so much the kind of loud judgment that points out a bad outfit or criticizes the local government handling of public transit. The judgment we want to look at is instant and already built into the thought.

For example, "I feel the wind" is an observation. On the other hand, "This damn wind is ruining my hair!" or "What a nice breeze!" are judgmental thoughts. The fact that the wind is blowing is already built into the thought.

Is judgment a bad thing? Not really. For one, it is unavoidable. Our egos are a big part of us, and it rules its little world by judging everything all the time. However, emotionally charged, negative judgment, and especially constant negative judgment—those thoughts that either remain in our heads or come out—can point to a lot of what's wrong with our lives, mainly pain.

Tied at the hip, negative judgment and pain take turns occupying the conscious mind and each invites the other when one leaves. This ties directly to previous discussions about creating reality. Events in our lives are objective—they are neither good nor bad. This is not to say that some events won't make you feel bad, but assigning a "bad event" label to an event is subjective because someone else might like something that you can't stand.

When we judge an event as negative and place strong emotions behind it, we pull one or two aspects of it that we don't like, and focus our attention on them. This causes the subconscious to understand what we prefer. Remember, the subconscious can, and does, make anything happen. It just needs direction, which we convey when we point to a negative aspect of an event. You say, "I don't like this part of that event." Your subconscious hears, "Generate more events that feel like that."

2. OUR OBSERVER

Nonjudgmental observation of thoughts is a powerful tool. For example, a thought comes by and says, "The train is late; it means you'll be late for dinner. This totally sucks!" You can stop at this point and think, "I just had a judgmental thought." You can observe it without judgment and then reevaluate it. "It's true that I will be late for dinner, but it's not such a big deal, and besides, I can't control the train so I might as well catch up on some reading (or writing)!"

This would be your observer talking. This is the real you—the one setting the grand agenda. The one painting the big picture before it becomes reality. The "real you" knows that everything in the world will turn out just fine and that living in the moment means nothing bad can happen.

THOUGHTS THAT COME FROM YOU

As we have just seen, another source of the thoughts floating in your head comes from you. If the other part is your subconscious, then the real you can be called *your consciousness.* Some refer to this part of you as *The Observer,* as it observes your life, events and the universe and reflects on them.

During precious instances throughout the day or week, you will actually have thoughts that come from this real you: aware, quietly observant, reflective thoughts that don't have judgment in them and that know that everything is good as it is.

One of the functions of those moments is to gently ask you where you want to go and in what direction you want to take your life. Many times those thoughts are swallowed in the constant noise of worldly, reality thoughts such as, "Why is the driver in front of me not driving a little faster?" or "Damn, I picked the slow cashier, again!" I am not suggesting that your brain shuts down and is completely quiet, but you can recognize those cherished times because you are actually reflecting on the big picture rather than being tied up in knots about life's drama or being in the middle of doing something.

Here, I would like to focus a specific event that repeats once in a while. It is a direction-request posed by your subconscious. It comes in the form of "What can I do to move toward my goal?" It can be general or aimed at any specific goal or desire you have.

You have just been given the floor during the planning committee meeting. The big question is, what are you going to say or do?

Remember, this is a fleeting moment. In no more than a few minutes, your subconscious is going to take over again, and you will be thrown right back into life's drama. Knowing how to rise to such occasions is important, since these are the rare times that you can actually steer your life in the right direction.

The first requirement for taking advantage of an opportunity is to know it's there in the first place. By simply reading this book, you will start to be aware of these openings when you are aware of your role in creating. You will notice the possibility to determine the course of your life.

The subconscious handles some things quite well on its own, such as breathing or chewing food. It can be useful to observe as you perform those functions, but sooner or later, you will realize that the subconscious is doing a good job and doesn't need to be monitored.

3. THE UNIVERSE

It seems to be tough for most people to believe the idea that we are somehow connected to the universe and to one another other in ways other than the "five scientifically proven" senses. I hear many reservations about this idea, with some pointing out that it has not been scientifically proven.

I'm not sure how many scientific journals those people read on a regular basis, or maybe they are just waiting for an edition of Time Magazine to come out with a big title that says, "Sixth Sense Finally Proven Beyond Doubt—It's No Longer Only for the Delusional!"

Luckily, science is much more advanced than public opinion, and more scientists are making amazing discoveries in that field. We forget that the everyday things we all take for granted rely on merely circumstantial evidence. Take gravity, for example. We all know it's there, but no one to date has any idea what causes it! Using the tools we possess today, there is no sign of the particle that interacts with gravity. Maybe we should start doubting that gravity exists altogether. Actually, many scientists believe that gravity is so weak because it exists on a different dimension and loses most of its power by the time it is felt on our dimension. Sounds a bit out of this world, doesn't it? We know about a fraction of what there is to know, and what we do know is marred by our beliefs.

There is no doubt in my mind that although we may not be yet able to measure or decipher the waves that are passed between people, their friends, and the universe, they do exist, and they play a huge role in our lives.

THE UNIVERSE TALKS

There are a few reasons why we can't hear the universe talk to us. First, there's a lot of noise in there! First, in the minds of most people, there's such a constant level of internal dialog that the thoughts that direct us so wisely are either not heard or are disregarded.

Second, universal inspiration comes in the form of thoughts, so it is not so easy to separate from our normal thoughts. Even though these inspirations give us priceless insight into things that we could be doing to improve our lives, they just get swallowed in a whirlwind of "urgent" thoughts and other things that we feel we must do.

Third, many of us so strongly believe that this possibility of connectedness does not exist that we wouldn't see it if it hit us on the head.

Once you let go of old beliefs, align yourself with your goals, and make that spiritual mumbo-jumbo part of your life, your communication with the universe will improve. You'll start getting a lot more of those universe thoughts and start to identify them and listen to them. In fact, you don't at all have to acknowledge, prove, or believe the source of those thoughts. Once you're at a point where they get your attention, and you actually act on them, they will be responsible for a good part of your success.

Those thoughts make you flip through the paper to the right ad, and they point out the person that, unlike your three previous boyfriends, will actually make you happy. It will point you, one at a time, to the endless string of opportunities that open in front of you all the time.

Although these thoughts flow through your head on a regular basis, it takes some work and some time until they can be heard and followed.

CHAPTER 6

The Ego, Subconscious, and Us

Until now, we talked about the subconscious and its role. We have hardly talked about another aspect of our existence: the ego. I will define these three aspects of our existence.

At our core, we are spiritual beings. We are deeply connected to everything in the universe and to other people. This is just our core, though; it is the soft, sweet, brilliant, and beautiful center we all possess. That's right. If you're human, you have it in you.

When we are conceived and later born to become a part of the physical world, we are unprotected from the vast range of experiences we encounter. It doesn't matter if our early experience is soft and caring or harsh and abrasive, one thing is common to all: our spiritual core is hurt and needs protection. This protection is separate from our parents and our environment—it comes from somewhere inside us. It protects us and keeps us safe by enacting a set of reactions and behaviors that encase our soft core with a harder shell. The more we are hurt, the harder and thicker the shell will be. This subconscious defense mechanism becomes our external self and is otherwise known as the ego.

In a way, we are all born with a dual personality: who we really are and who our ego is. The ego, our protector, is far beyond our years. It can grasp the world and knows what reactions to develop to protect us from our bad experiences coming back and hurting us again. Being a part of the subconscious, it possesses some great powers.

This ego defense system, however, comes with a high price tag. It forms protective habits that become so ingrained into how we think and act that we might think that they are an inseparable part of who we are. We learn very early that it is always safe to identify with that ego: it always has answers and can get us back to our comfort zones. Even after the protection offered is no longer required, we still cannot easily free ourselves from old habits.

But what can be that wrong with a defensive lifestyle? What's wrong with having a comfort zone and sticking to it? If your comfort zone is being happy, relaxed, and content, then nothing is wrong. In fact, we want our comfort zones to be a comfortable place to be. For most of us, however, it is anything but. Our comfort zones are usually not aligned with what we want for ourselves. For most of us, it's much more comfortable being unsuccessful, not having money, and not being in shape. In those cases, the ego will protect us by making us feel bad. It may not be fun, but it is safe.

We even know to say when the ego is hurt, yet we can't separate it from us. We identify with the ego to such a degree that when it tells us we're hurting, we feel it and can't easily get out of it. Let's look at a typical example, and if this is not the case with you, you can relate to similar examples.

Imagine that you're driving down the road and another driver cuts you off. Your ego tells you, "Hey, this guy was rude to us, and we feel down." So, you feel down for twenty or thirty minutes, or it might actually ruin your day. Logically this doesn't make any sense. You don't know that person in the other car, and whatever they did has nothing to do with how you feel. After all, they didn't stab you, curse your mother by her first name, or unload a pile of rocks that dented your car. Your encounter had no lasting meaning other than you feeling bad.

You feel bad because ego told you to feel bad, and you identified with it. There was no choice there. If you sat at home and I came in and told you to be hurt, would you just be hurt? Would you turn a perfectly good day into a bad day just because I said so? Most likely, you would turn to me with half a smile, saying something like, "Ahhh...and why should I feel bad, again?"

When the ego tells us we're feeling bad, we do not question the circumstances, we just agree and feel bad. The first thing we will learn to do with the ego is question it. We will question it every time we feel bad. Why? Because of a very important rule we have yet to discuss. It is so simple, making it impossible to forget, and yet it will probably throw off some serious alarms for you. The rule is this: *everything is always as it should be in the world.* That's right. Regardless of how we feel, all is as it should be.

Now, if you are like most other people, the first things that come to mind are some hypothetical worst-case scenarios. Or maybe you relate it to things that happened to you, such as, "How can everything be okay in the world when people you love die?" It is tough to answer, but let me try. First, in an average life there are only a handful of situations where people you love die. When you have a good life, you have people you love, and some will die before you. We know that death is an inevitable part of life. Regardless, we feel terrible when it happens to someone we love. I don't expect you to feel good at that moment, but I do expect you to question and observe the many times you feel bad during the day, week, or month that don't have a tragic reason. It's more an everyday life thing rather than a big, sad event.

Once we realize that despite feeling bad, sometimes things are as they should be, we can tweak it into a more personal message: *everything always turns out good for me*. What you may notice is that these two phrases are the exact opposite of what your ego is constantly telling you. Instead, the ego is full of warnings and cautionary tales:

"Be careful here!"

"Ooh, don't get into that."

"Now we don't know what is going to happen…"

"How will I ever get this done in time?"

Since your ego's job is to be your protector, it's no wonder that it bases most of its language on fear and anxiety. As you gain practice, you will learn to catch your ego as it makes an effort to keep you "safe." The difference is going to be your response. Instead of buying into the warnings and the doom scenarios presented, you will say, "Thanks, but I made up my mind to be happy right now, and besides, everything always turns out just fine."

Eventually habits will start to change and the "feel bad" cues you'll get will be further apart. You will feel bad less and feel good more, which is, by our earlier definition, a better life.

To be distinguished from the ego, the subconscious is the powerful "software" connecting our minds (the observer), the ego (the subconscious creation), and the universe at large.

The subconscious is the mechanism that makes everything in our lives happen. It has an incomprehensible capacity to make calculations, extrapolate information, and be in tune with our bodies, minds, souls, and senses (and I do mean all six). You can say that the sixth sense is our connection with the universe we discussed earlier.

THINGS WE CONTROL

Although our ability to control various aspects of our lives is limited, one of the things we can control is how we feel. Interestingly, the control over how we feel is something we like to disassociate from. You feel how you feel, how can you control it? Well, you can't always prevent bad feelings from washing over you, but you can tweak them once they do. Give it a shot right now: imagine something in your life that is working well, even if you have to stretch a bit. Then take that good feeling and feel good about feeling good. We will talk more about the importance of feeling good later in the book, but for now, it is important to realize that how you feel doesn't have to be the result of an event outside of you. It can also be a result of a simple decision to choose to feel good right now.

Gratitude is another emotion you can control. Feeling grateful is one of the most powerful tools for creating good things in your life. At any point during the day when you remember reading this, you can't do more positive things for your life than to find something to feel grateful for.

THE ORDER OF THINGS

One aspect of the difficulty we face when attempting to better our lives has to do with our perception of cause and effect. For the most part, we simply have it all wrong.

For example, take the commonly used expression, “I’ll believe it when I see it.” This is the phrase of the ultra-realist, the one with his or her feet planted in the ground and his or her head in the real world. It is a notion held by those who objectively analyze events as they come and make scientifically based decisions.

While I fully appreciate the need some have to see evidence before embracing an idea, when it comes to changing our lives, it is a complete impossibility. Being unable to believe something until it is seen is a self-imposed mental disability. The simple fact is that we cannot see, let alone make happen, anything we do not believe in. Let’s take a pragmatic look at this.

If I say, “I saw a flying purple cow,” and you say, “I’ll believe it when I see it,” well, neither of us is constrained in any way since the existence of purple cows is irrelevant. However, when the matter is making your life better and getting you to be happier and have more of what you want, believing has to come first. In this case, if you decide to wait until you see things are better before you can believe that they are, you will suffer the unfortunate side effects of a long and frustrating status quo.

Let’s look at the order of things and see how we can turn belief into a powerful tool without needing to believe crazy things. An unwillingness to believe things that are yet to exist can be a major obstacle when we want to make life changes. If I tell you that you can have a million dollars next week, you can either believe or not. It has no real consequence since the idea didn’t come from you. But what about your internal dialog—what about things you want but refuse to believe are possible? What if you have your own “million-dollar” things you wish you had, such as someone to love (who will, this time, love you back), financial independence, or anything else that looks unrealistic. What if you wanted to work doing what you love? If I told you that it is all possible, and you said, "I'll believe it when I see it," or "It's not realistic," then that will be very unfortunate for you. Nothing in your life happens unless you believe it can happen, and this strong belief that you are on your merry way there, wherever it may be, is the single strongest moving and changing force in your universe. Your reality mimics your vision. If you can't mentally see yourself in the situation you want, the chances of it becoming a part of *your* reality are slim to none.

While some people will tell you that visualizing yourself as you want to be is easy, I can tell you that it is not. It may actually go right up against some deeply ingrained habits you formed.

That the kind of belief we're looking at here is not something we can simply tell ourselves we believe. It may be a start, but some beliefs, negative or positive, are deeply ingrained in our personalities. Rather than seeing them as beliefs, we simply see them as *the way things are.*

Another aspect of cause and effect that you may be interested in is the revolutionary findings that scientists are making in the field of quantum physics. What they are finding out is that cause and effect is not linear as we thought. The old Newtonian cause and effect paradigm that states that event A causes event B, which will then cause event C, is proven as not true. Instead, many factors come together to form a single result.

There are many examples where our perception of cause and effect hinders our ability to change. Dating, weight loss, a work situation, money—all are affected. For example, many of us are looking for what we don't have right now and live under the self-imposed rule that we will be happy once we have what we want. The self-talk consists of saying, "I will be happy when I am dating someone I love," or "I will be happy when I am thin." After all, if dating is what you're lacking in life and otherwise you're lonely, how can you be happy until you find that love?

Let me ask you another question: Who in their right mind would want to date an unhappy person? Are you looking for someone who's unhappy? Nope, you are looking for a confident, self-sufficient, happy person to love. Guess what? As long as you are unhappy about your situation, regardless of what it is, that situation is not going to change. Period. If your stance is that you will be happy when (fill in the blank), then etch this truth into your thick, stubborn mind: it will never happen.

Please know that this was not meant as an insult. Most people, including me, have a thick, stubborn mind. This is why our issues are so universal, and we all have a hard time breaking out and making lasting positive changes.

But the other side of that story is really good! Once we change the way we see the world, flipping cause and effect over on its head, life will instantly change. No, I am not suggesting that you will fall right to the center of the weight chart and into the center of attention of your previously unaware love interest. I am saying that seeing things differently can make us feel good right away, and feeling good is the one true measure of a good life. Once we feel good, changes in our life situation will follow.

Assume that you are unhappy with some aspects of your life. At this point, they are the focus of your life. Instead of having those in the to-change list, these aspects are ruling your mood and therefore your life. What you have to understand is that having things we don't like is not who we are. Those things are not life; they are only a part of the current life situation. What makes those things bad is a constant negative focus on them.

Imagine this: *whatever we want is waiting to become a part of our reality.* Waiting for what? For us to stop resisting it! This is not blaming or saying your situation is your fault. It's just saying that *things are now up to you.*

The world is full of everything we want. It may seem like you're on a different dimension since people you could be dating are passing by you all the time and never seem to notice you. You see and hear about tons of money exchanging hands every day, although none of it seems to end up in your bank account. And if your weight is the issue? Healthy eating choices are everywhere and opportunities to live actively are as accessible as opening your front door. Besides, you lose weight every minute of every day; it is just that you're also gaining weight. What you want is right here, right around you, within your reach all the time. You know that, which makes it that much more frustrating.

The lack of opportunities is not responsible for whatever we lack. It is unknowingly resisting, avoiding, fearing, or altogether not seeing these opportunities. Deep-rooted beliefs contrary to what those opportunities can bring prevent us from seeing the opportunities. Viewing life negatively and focusing on what we don't have prevent us from acting on opportunities.

I'm not saying that it is easy or blaming you for anything that is wrong in your life, or for causing your own mess. I am just telling you that it is your own frustration that blocks the goodness that is knocking at your door every day.

After hearing this, There are two possible responses to this:

1. The mean writer blames me for my bad luck—what an idiot.

2. Oh, my life can really change! If it is up to me to make my life good, and this nice guy will give me some starting tips, then this is really possible! It is now up to you to determine a direction.

Everything we are looking at here is leading toward one assertion, which is something that can be as scary as it is exhilarating. The sticky notion is that something within us creates our own reality.

Our life situation, in its entirety, is a reflection of who we are. It reflects our beliefs, our fears, and how we see ourselves. Our reality today is a continuously choreographed number, planned by our thoughts and intentions some weeks ago, while providing material for the acts of the coming weeks.

The idea that we are not only responsible for the consequence of our actions but also that our actions, reactions, thoughts and beliefs are the matter of which reality is composed can be tough to swallow. Even if part of us understands, and we theoretically agree with it, there will always be a part of us that doubts that. For one, it should not make total sense to us that our lives are choreographed. It is more natural for us to believe that life happens. We're raised to believe that the random sum of everything that's going on makes life what it is. The other aspect is that the ego's job is to protect us from the awful guilt we would feel if we accepted that we created everything in our lives. This is something that is stronger for some, easier to accept for others, and completely impossible for still others to comprehend. For some, the idea that they somehow have a hand in the negative aspects of their lives is so threatening that the ego will take over whenever that idea is suggested.

Regardless, a part of each of us knows that. A part of us, the same part that knows that all is well in the world regardless of how we feel sometimes, knows that the key to reality-creation is in us. Accepting that fact is a necessary step in making positive, long lasting changes in life.

Whether you are able to use that understanding to spark change is encoded in you somewhere. Go figure it out.

RECONCILING A ROUGH START

A recurring theme I hear when talking about creating our own reality is about children. How can it be true that we create our own reality when a baby is born with a disease or poverty? Did that baby create his tough start in life?

No. We all have a starting point, and some more advantageous, some less. When you were born, you already had various conditions imposed based on your circumstances.

The nine months you spent in your mother's womb is possibly the biggest contributor to how good a start one has in life. If you believe that the first few years of a person's life are formative, think about the first few months after conception. The baby is literally formed. Anything from the mother's nutrition to the stress she is feeling to sounds the baby hears can have a tremendous effect on the baby's growth and development.

For some people, it is possible that having a bad start seals the deal and emotionally recovering from it is impossible. I urge you to differentiate the bad start you may have had as a child at a time where you were unable to make any decisions from where you are now as a grown-up. Remember that blaming your life situation on your childhood is detrimental to moving forward.

I was put in a children's house on a Kibbutz in Israel when I was only three days old. I am certain that getting so little physical contact at that young age really messed me up on many levels. I could just look at it as irreversible damage that was done to me. Instead of casting blame, I rebuilt the damaged pieces the best I could and am still working on it. I did it using the very techniques described in this book, and while the side effects of that bad start will never really go away, they are no longer a cause of pain in my life.

BEYOND SELF-HELP

It is quite possible that for some people, it's too late for a self-help book, or at least it can't be the only method for turning a life around. There are many ways to jump-start change or make a mental difference using external methods rather than solely relying on our own minds to help us. Regardless, the concepts are similar. Something within will have to be aware enough to seek this help, and a switch has to be flipped for us to move from the "life sucks and it's other people's fault" state to "it can be salvaged, and I am in charge."

There is no real difference between reading a self-help book and committing yourself to the psych ward for evaluation. Any time you decide to seek help to make things better in your life, it counts. No matter what your condition is, moving forward is always the right direction, and it always takes something inside to spark the change.

HAPPY-SEEING

This is a good time to move forward with some ideas and understand them a bit better so that we can eventually move toward the how-to portion of the book. What we have seen so far is that focusing on the negative aspect of events in our lives is mostly habitual and done subconsciously. Most important, it blocks the flow of good things.

If that is the case, then what is the alternative? Focusing on positive things that don't really exist? Isn't seeing negative things that are actually there more realistic than focusing on the good things that aren't real?

Being happy about being thin while you are obviously overweight is delusional, and pretending you have money when you don't can be depressing. So where does seeing the positive fit in, and how can it be done?

Wanting to be realistic is one thing, but having that realistic view of the world bring on negative emotions and negative consequences is another thing that we have to discuss. You can be in a negative situation while not being unhappy or depressed. You can be stuck on the side of the highway, be late for work, have no cell phone, and still be fully in the moment. You may not be the happiest you've ever been, but you also don't have to have the sense of despair and frustration. You can still know that life is good.

As an example, let's use a weight problem. You can substitute any problem you perceive to have in your life at present. If you are overweight, your weight may be on your mind a lot of the time. Thinking about your ongoing difficulty with losing weight can't make you happy.

I am not sure how else to say it other than just come out and say it: feeling bad about your weight sends instructions to your subconscious to keep you fat and bring you back to that feeling of despair. Your only chance of permanently changing your life is by feeling good, regardless of your current reality.

This may seem like another line in the book you can just skim over and move on to something more pleasant to read. It is not. This idea is so fundamental to you overcoming what life is throwing at you right now that I will be repeating it again here and throughout this book. So, here goes again. Read this and start to internalize: the only way out of a bad situation is by feeling good.

This is not to say that it's easy to do, especially not in the long term. If we could flip a switch and just feel good because that's how we were built, then all our problems would be over, and we would just feel good.

Our human condition, however, makes long-term positive change a bit more difficult to bring about. We have to think in ways that defy logic. We are required to have a state of mind we aren't used to having. Being happier starts with being uncomfortable.

THE OTHER FEEL GOOD

If feeling good is all it takes, then couldn't we just all get high and be done with it? When you're unhappy, if a cigarette resolves it and you feel better, why is it not a solution?

There are shortcuts to feeling good, but they always have a down side. Unlike the pure joy of feeling good from inside, using external means of feeling good, such as drugs and alcohol, eating, shopping, or whatever else we're addicted to, can only delay the bad feeling. It not only delays feeling bad, but also compresses and concentrates it, so that we're less likely understand how to deal with it and more likely to return to the same methods of extinguishing pain.

So how can we differentiate between the *feel good* that comes from simply being in the moment and the *feel good* we get from smoking or eating a cookie? The difference is very simple: one kind of feeling good brings on more feeling good. The other one, eventually, will bring on bad feelings that will be more powerful that the good you felt initially.

One of the interesting things with drugs is that some will actually cause the same reaction as a deep spiritual experience. So what is the difference? Mental readiness. Imagine that you just got a membership to the gym because you want really defined, muscular arms. You go to the gym and there are several rooms in a row. You are told to start with room one, and after some time of using the light weights there, move to room two, and then three, and on.

After a few days, you notice that the arms of the people leaving room ten are the way you wish your arms would look. So you jump right to room ten and lift some of the weights. Like magic, your arms buff up, and you leave happy. The next morning, though, you realize that you can't move your arms at all, and you are completely out of commission for a week. You pushed yourself too hard, and your body was not ready. Like lifting weights, your mind and soul have to be ready for a deep spiritual experience before the benefits can be reaped. Taking drugs will get you there for a moment, but the down side is going to be more awful than you can imagine.

CHAPTER 7

The Flow and the Ego

Let's talk about reality as it relates to the universe. The flow is a common and effective term used to describe the universe and our lives. You may have heard about it at some point. In any case, here's my take.

The flow describes the universe as it relates to life. In that analogy, the flow is where things are good and where we want to be. I like to call the flow *the current*, since being in the current can also mean being saturated in what is happening now.

The flow never stops and being in it is always good. The important thing is our relation to the flow: we are either in it, partially in it, or not in it at all. While we cannot block the flow itself, we certainly can block ourselves from being in the flow.

You may be able to recall being in the flow at some point. Everything goes right, life at the moment is effortless, and things just click. The main thing, I think, about being in the flow is that you feel good, and when you feel good, life is good.

We are in the flow when we are doing something we really love. It can be playing the cello or playing baseball with your kids.

It can be negotiating a million-dollar real estate deal or negotiating the forest floor for a place to plant your tent for the night. Since we are all different, different activities put us in the flow.

In the flow, we can almost feel a flow of good energy running through us. There's no stress or worry; there's no feeling that we should be somewhere else or do anything else.

Much of what we discuss in this book relates to being in the flow, whether I specifically mention it or not. Recognizing the flow and knowing when we're not in it is important, even if we don't see a quick way to get back into it.

We will return to discussing the flow as we see how we can make positive changes in our lives. For now, I want to introduce you to a little trick I devised for getting back into the flow. I call this the *magic question*, and it works really well with practice. Whenever you sense anxiety or frustration with a situation, ask yourself: *Is there anything I can or am willing to do right now to resolve the situation?*

If the answer is *yes*, do it right at that moment. If the answer is no, simply forget about it. Just like that. Let it go. Holding onto an anxious thought does nothing to resolve the issue and keeps you out of the flow. The next time anxiety washes over you, take this trick for a spin and test your ability to let go of a menacing thought.

THE VALUE OF NOT DOING

Many times, we become anxious because we feel that we are not doing enough to move things forward, whatever those things may be—work, love, career, sales, fitness, etc. Many self-help books say taking action is a key ingredient to success. If we don't do things, how can we expect them to happen?

The truth is, when it is right to do something, and that thing is going to move us forward, action is not going to come out of anxiety. Doing things just because we feel anxious about not moving forward is almost guaranteed to mess things up more. When we are in the flow and our wants are aligned with our beliefs, we will do things effortlessly. When you believe you can be fit, you will find yourself working out. When you believe you're not bound to walking a financial tightrope, you will find yourself making meaningful career moves. When you believe that you are worthy of a mate, you will find yourself talking to suitable people. None of those actions will come out of the anxious need to move things forward.

CYCLE OF CREATION AND BELIEF

Earlier in the book, we discussed the cycle of reality regeneration, which is the idea that our life situation is directed like a play, and while characters are allowed to ad-lib, we are the ones setting the direction. Let's take a closer look at this idea.

The reality we live in is not static and is certainly not predetermined. Reality is being constantly generated. The plans for building reality are in beliefs, affirmations, and focus. While we don't really control any of the details of everyday life, we can have a profound impact on the plan that does. Since everyday life, including our reactions and actions, is in line with that blueprint, we direct life by constantly drawing and redrawing the plan.

If you like your life the way it is, changing the plan is not needed. Your subconscious is doing its job in maintaining life on the same level and keeping it in the same direction.

But when you want to change your life—and therefore parts of the plan—you suddenly encounter a conflicting situation: your plan calls for one thing, but you get something else because your life is still using the old plan.

For example, let's say that you decided to get fit, and you are going through the right motions of visualizing. Your plan will start to be rewritten, but your subconscious is still using the old parts of the plan, so it will push you to watch TV instead of working out.

This happens because implementing a new plan can take some time. It can be a short amount of time, or it can take years. While there is no set time for new intentions to take, about a month or two is a reasonable amount of time to expect.

Let's look at another example for this. Imagine that you are the CEO of a fast-food franchise company. Your company has been running for years to the point where it is running itself, and you don't need to do much. One day you get up and decide that you will introduce a new sandwich that will have the cheese under the burger. This idea is very much within the original premise, but it will still take a couple of weeks to create the marketing, teach the staff to make the new sandwich, change the menus, etc. There will be a delay between your inspiration and the final product being changed. Using this analogy, the final product is your life or your reality.

What if you, the CEO, had a different idea: you want to change the entire franchise from unhealthy, fast food to a raw health food chain instead. This is such a big change, it is quite possible that your board of directors or stockholders will give you the boot and fire you. Instead of dropping the bomb publicly, you decide to start a slow, cultural change. You want everyone working for you, from your close advisors all the way to the servers, to understand the importance of serving healthy food. This scenario is much more feasible, but you can see that it will take a lot of time, and until the entire organization, top to bottom, is behind the idea, implementation will be tough and will meet a lot of resistance.

Changes on a personal level work very much the same way. Since we have so many layers imprinted with our beliefs and habits, making a sweeping change means having to reimprint every bit of you with new ideas. It's like creating a new menu for yourself, featuring healthy food rather than junk food.

The effort it takes to make lasting, meaningful changes in our lives is not comfortable effort to take on. It's not like climbing a mountain or powering through a long workday. Making change happen requires us to change the part that does most of our thinking, which is why it can be difficult and is rather rare when it works. Even when we decide to make a significant change and succeed to some degree, it can be a month, a year, or longer before our old self catches up with us, and we're dragged back to old habits in the meantime. This is because the change did not go all the way through you. There were parts still imprinted with old beliefs, and like a volcano, they lay dormant until one day they found a crack and erupted.

NATURAL SHORTCUTS

Sometimes, extreme situations cause a profound change in our consciousness. I'm sure you've heard of people who went through a near-death experience, lost a family member, or had a major scare in a form of a disease or injury. Due to the extreme event, their ego gives way to a deeper understanding of their existence. Their outlook on the world changes, their priorities shift, and they seem to be more enlightened. This is because they are. In a funny way, those people will go on having a better life.

Eckhart Tolle, the esteemed writer of *The Power of Now* and *A New Earth*, describes how his miserable, egocentric life abruptly changed one day when his ego was simply stripped off. He became, to his amazement, enlightened in a single moment. He then spent some years homeless, wandering around marveling at the beauty of life. Can you imagine? A homeless man who lost everything being happier and more at peace than you and I will ever be.

Another good story is the one of Aron Ralston, who, while hiking in Utah, managed to get his arm trapped under a rock. To free himself, he was forced to cut his arm off with a dull knife. Aron is now a motivational speaker. It seems that what should have been a devastating experience has freed more than his body.

Extreme, painful events can be called life-changing events for a reason. Either they push us deeper into a victim state, or they reset our priorities and lift the awful rule of the ego, replacing it with an enlightened state of being.

So does becoming more enlightened require a traumatic, potentially life-threatening event? While it is certainly a short-cut, much like an earthquake can give you a head start on that complete house renovation you intended to get to for years, it is not the only way. The alternative as I see it is to slowly shift your priorities and increase your consciousness. It is possible, but you will face stiff resistance from your subconscious. This resistance will not be easy to recognize. You will not be lucky to be thinking, "You can't make a positive change, so sit down, because being a loser is great!" Instead, your ego has much more tricky ways, such as inserting discouraging thoughts to your head that you actually believe are your own.

The ability to allow is the main skill we need to develop. This is seeing the good in the world as the flow, where we don't need to struggle but rather just be a part of what is. As people, we are good at either winning or losing. We find the letting go part near impossible.

OUR FOCUS

Focus is one aspect of our existence that can predict the direction we're headed. Focus is what we see during the day and what we pay attention to. We already discussed the idea that reality is not life as we know it, but it is rather a tiny, subjective segment of all there is. As long as we live in this world, we will never be able to see more than just a fraction of everything that is going on. That's a good thing, because if we did experience more than this fraction, we would experience such an overload that we would most certainly lose it.

Our ego, however, likes to tell us otherwise. The ego tells us that the world's reality is just what we see, hear, and read about in the paper. It has us believe that we know what is going on.

Our narrow focus has a practical function. Our conscious minds are far too slow to process the massive amount of information required for us to do even the most basic things. But our specific focus reveals a deeper truth about our human condition. Our focus shows us the few things around us that match what we already know and believe.

The first thing you need come to terms with is that your reality is just that: *your reality.* It is not mine; it is not your friend's, co-worker's, spouse's, or anyone else's.

Our reality is made of things we pay attention to, and things we pay attention to make up what we focus on. Our focus is much like the main theme of a TV channel. The focus of the History Channel, for example, is history shows. However, they do have shows about loosely related subjects, such as finding Bigfoot. But even when not all shows are about World War II or ancient Greece, the feel of the channel and its identity remains true to the main theme. If the station wanted to shift its focus to, say, politics, it could only do that by examining the lineup and switching shows.

The same is true with us. Things we focus on during the day reflect our beliefs and our points of view. They also, for the most part, determine what we think about and how we view and interpret events in our lives. Changing life, or a part of it, has to include seriously examining our thoughts. We need to review the schedule of thoughts and reactions we have throughout the day.

This is a three-step process. The first thing we have to come to terms with is the scope of our vision. We need to accept that our reality is so subjective and tightly focused that it is not *reality* but is rather as unique as we are. This can be difficult if you pride yourself, as many do, on being *realistic*. If you believe yourself to be realistic, but reality is not truly a universal thing, then you must have been fooling yourself. I can tell you with a distinct certainty that you have been. The faster you learn that it's not a big deal and get over it, the faster you'll be able to move on to the next step.

The second step is to realize what our focus is. When we live all our lives believing that our reality is just reality, we lose the ability to recognize our own subjectivity. Our beliefs tint most of our thoughts. Analyzing these thoughts and gaining an insight to the tint they share will reveal your very own reality check.

The common tint thoughts share can reflect the many unknown things that you should know about yourself.

The third step is observing the focus we have. When I started analyzing my own focus, I was stunned to realize what utterly pointless things were coloring (tinting) my thoughts. When I started writing down what I believed was the focus of each batch of thoughts, I could see the color of the filter I was seeing the world through.

This focus is not the subject of the thoughts. As people living in the same country, most of us have thoughts that generally fit the same general subjects: family, politics, sex, work, money, sex, hobby, art, sex, etc. What matters here is the tint or twist we put on our thoughts.

For example, a tint can be how much better you are than anyone else at anything or how you're always the victim in a situation. It can be related to what others think of you, which is a tint beloved by many egos. The tint can be related to gender or ethnicity, and many thoughts can be colored with "I am Italian," "I am a woman," etc.

Just realizing and observing our focus can explain a lot about life. Focus is not just a side effect or peripheral fun fact about your life. It shapes our lives. Focus gives meaning to events in our lives and gives the events context. The judgment that we place on pieces of our daily life will be recorded and remembered for future events. By now, this judgment is so ingrained that it no longer takes any thinking, and it is not easily visible. It seems like a natural part of our lives.

The judgment is not a bad thing by default, but the flavor of that judgment gives our lives its taste and makes future events what they are.

If, for example, you see many events in your life as it relates to you being screwed, then your subconscious will seek more of those events and instances. On the other hand, the focus we have can be a thick mask whose purpose is to hide from us what we find most painful. For example, a tint that we are superior to others could have been your subconscious method of masking a deep sense of low self-worth. The problem is that like every mask, this mask has to come off once in a while, and these times can be saturated with pain.

It can also very well be that your focus is so deep that your subconscious will simply not allow you to see it. This is the case with people who often identify with the fact that they know the truth. They believe their judgment of events, siding with one element against another element, is the ultimate truth. In their minds, the world is divided into those who agree with them and those who don't. It can be very difficult for people like that to grasp that the big picture is much more complicated, and that their truth is just, well, *their* truth.

Another level of focused control is when focus not only tints a person's thoughts, but also becomes the intense subject of the thoughts. For example, people with OCD have constant thoughts whose tint doesn't have to be deciphered because it is right there. "I need to wash my hands." There is no tint; it's just only the subject of the thought.

Okay, so it's assignment time. (Do this only if you think it can be a fun thing). Take a notebook with you for the day, and write down the focus of your thoughts. The focus I am looking for here is the moral of the thought, not so much the actual subject. I am looking for the manner in which the thought relates to you personally and the way the thought relates to how you feel at the time and why.

Try to find the common thread of your thoughts. It is there, and it is clearly marked. The only reason it's difficult to see is that your ego is hiding it from you. Take a light approach to it and see it as a fun game, and you'll have a better chance.

WHAT OTHERS THINK

Our perception of what others think of us is one of the more universal and detrimental thought focuses we can have. This type of thought is such a universal part of our egos that very few people can claim that they don't stumble on that thought at least weekly. For others, it can be a debilitating condition.

These thoughts come in two flavors: what others think of us and what others might think about us. For most of us, the aspect of what others think about us or what they might think if we do or say this or that is but a thin, murky film on our daily lives. It's like an invisible wet blanket protecting us from exploring our potential. Since this blanket has been there from a young age, you may be just dismissing it as one of the hidden costs of being alive. Worrying what others will think is a part of reality that when we happen to notice in ourselves, we just take as a necessary evil. We may believe that the course of our lives is determined by the hypothetical other people—people who may hire us, invite us to the coveted garden party, tell even a larger circle of yet more "other people" about what we did, and other life-wrecking, irreversible atrocities.

The "what people think" thing was a bit of a shock to me on my personal journey. I prided myself on not caring what anyone thinks. My focus, as I discovered when I examined my thoughts, was much different.

I came to realize that I used the "I don't care what people think" to mask my difficulty of dealing with emotional events. It became sort of a cool thing, where I pretended not to care—doing things that would either piss people off or just come off as odd, just to keep that facade going.

Once I realized that, I chose to sculpt it into a focus more in line with who I wanted to be.

I stopped saying, "I don't care," which truly meant, "I care deeply but have no ability to deal with it." I made an effort to notice when I am too involved in what someone thinks, which now gives me a strong indication to whether I am on the right track. It was almost like setting an alarm clock. I told myself that whenever an "I don't care" thought went through my head, I had to become aware. This worked quite well.

Since I could now recognize that focus and wake up when I sensed it coming, it was no longer an effective masking method for my ego. By now, it's far less prevalent. Instead of being a masking agent, it illuminates events in my life and gives me a better tool to know if I'm on the right path.

Here are a few facts we need to come to terms with regarding what other people think:

No matter what we do, some people will think good things, and some people will think bad things about us. Nothing you can do can change that. You can make the opinions more or less extreme, but people have their own focus and will have their opinions to match. This has very little to do with you, other than what is going in your own mind, which has everything to do with you.

We can still monitor and care what people think without having it change what we do.

Reveling in what others think is speculative and can be haunting, debilitating, constraining, and the cause of a lot of pain. Regardless, it is not something you can ever completely stop doing.

It is important to realize that there's nothing inherently wrong with contemplating what people think of this or that action. The important things are to evaluate whether these thoughts are obsessive or have a limiting effect on your life.

I believe it's important to realize on an intellectual level that for the most part, following your heart is better than going by what you believe people will think. When you follow your heart, other people who do the same—people of integrity with a tendency toward freedom—will most certainly recognize it. The result will be that they will think good things about you.

CHAPTER 8

Expectations

To achieve, you must have a goal, and as you strive toward that goal. Expectation, you may think, can help guide your way.
Think again.

THE KITCHEN TIMER

I came up with the kitchen timer analogy while driving. I was figuring out why we lose our patience during drives and why we wish we'd arrive already. So I thought about rides in which we don't lose our patience. For example, if you're driving from Providence, Rhode Island, to anywhere in Vermont, it takes at least three hours. I am guessing that people who don't suffer from a compulsive complaining disorder or from some physical pain can sit through most of this ride rather quietly. In the fourth hour, our patience will suddenly snap, we become antsy, and we wish we were no longer stuck in that car with those people.

This situation is understandable with long rides, but what about shorter rides? If we go on a forty-five-minute ride that is taking longer than expected, there's a good chance that after about an hour, we will again become restless.

But why? We are perfectly capable of sitting in a car for hours when we know in advance that the ride will be at least that long. It seems that when we are set to do a long and possibly boring task, we set our very own mental kitchen timer for about the time that activity was supposed to take. As soon as the timer goes off, we lose our patience.

The explanation was clear: when we are set to take on a task that includes waiting, we start to lose patience sometime before it ends. This is true regardless if the wait is three hours or thirty seconds.

Those times when we lose our patience are part of a greater picture, and as you will soon see, they also affect other parts of our lives.

EXPECTATIONS

The underlying issue with losing our patience and wanting to move to the next thing is tied to one thing: our expectations.

It makes no difference if it's a forty-minute drive, a wait at the line in the store, or during a phone call that interrupts our TV show. When we set our expectations to a specific outcome at a specific time, and that outcome isn't met in time, there will be frustration.

This setup is not constrained to things we can time. Consider the following: any time we believe we have a problem, the cause is not the event or situation itself. There is often a disparity between the event itself and the expectation of how things should have gone down.

Why do things you consider to be a problem have no emotional effect on someone else? Some people explain their troubles to you and you have to sympathize, but you really think, "This is not really a problem." Why?

Because there is never a problem that is not someone's problem. Even the dictionary defines a problem as "a source of perplexity, distress, or vexation." This means that if no one finds a situation perplexing, distressful, or causing vexation, there is no problem. In other words, a problem only exists if we call it a problem.

Okay, so it's not so simple. The judgment that an event is a problem and the resulting discomfort happen automatically. Before we even have a chance to evaluate a situation, the subconscious has activated the "problem" alert. It does that using our earlier reactions to similar events as a guide.

The victim that lives in each one of our egos to a varying degree has already jumped all over it and got its kicks. The part of us that needs problems found its outlet.

So as you see, the kitchen timer that tells us when it's a good time to start getting frustrated is only a small side effect of a bigger thing: the subconscious starting problems.

ELIMINATING PROBLEMS AT THE ROOT

A few things can help us deal with any problem much better. It's important to first understand that a problem is a good thing when it's not an emotional downer. For example, let's say that you have a problem. Your car is in the garage, and you need to get to work.

If it causes frustration, stress, and fears of all kinds, the cause for the bad time it is giving you is, well, you. You had no idea, so it's not really your fault. Regardless, your reaction to this event rather than the event itself causes frustration or pain in your life.

Granted, if you told your sob story to the first hundred people you met, most of them would tell you that indeed, you are the victim of circumstance and that your stress is warranted. It may feel good to be the victim in some way, to get some attention from people while we complain to them about our horrible morning. But this story has another side to it, and that other side is going to catch up with us. When we place emotional value on an event, we're giving the subconscious the direction to bring more events that cause us to feel that way. Am I saying that you brought this car thing on yourself in the first place? It's quite possible.

So how do we deal with upsetting events in a way that will not make way for more to come later? First, let's say that we're looking at mild to moderately upsetting events. If you come home and your dog is dead, you will be upset and there's not much you can or should do about it. However, most events that happen to us during the week, which we deem as problems, are subjective at most. We either invited these things in with our negative outlook or simply misjudged and made a big deal about. So, what we do is very simple: we observe and reflect.

OBSERVE OUR REACTIONS AND REFLECT ON THEM.

Right now, it's up to the subconscious to react for us. It is so used to the recipe we taught it of how we prefer to feel at different situations that it will make us feel that way. It will get us there regardless of our new intentions or how much we believe it's our choice not to get upset. Emotional habits are deeply ingrained and happen before we notice. However, as an event happens, and as we get upset, or sometime after, we can observe our reactions. We can tell ourselves, "Hey, I just had a totally benign event, and I got completely bent out of shape over it. That's kind of funny, my old habits."

Starting today, understand on an intellectual level that problems are rooted in your reactions to events, not the events themselves. On top of that, whenever you remember, tell yourself the following: *There are no problems in my life*, and, *everything in my life always works out great.* These affirmations, along with lighthearted observation, can be very powerful in starting to slowly change your automatic reaction.

Anxiety-inducing events call for a single yes/no question: Is there something I can, or am willing do right now to make things better? When the answer is yes, do it. Right away, with a smile, if possible. You did your thing. When the answer is no, get it out of your head as soon as you can. Example: It is Sunday afternoon, my car is in the garage, and I have no idea if it will be ready for tomorrow. How is this not stressful? Well, it is stressful if you become stressed. Let's see what can be done. You can't call the garage because they are closed. If you can think, right now, of another ride in case the car is not ready, make the phone call and arrange it. If you need to call someone at work to alert them that there's a possibility that you will be late, do it as soon as possible. Beyond that, there's nothing to do, so just let it go and enjoy your evening.

I realize that stressful situations like that can't just be neutralized at will. After all, that stressful feeling is the product of years of habit-forming reactions and thought patterns. However, the letting go process can start as soon as something clicks at your intellectual level.

A CASE AGAINST EXPECTATIONS

In a previous section, we discussed the contribution of expectations to what we call problems and to our level of stress, anxiety, etc. How we eventually feel dictates how the subconscious handles situations, not that it will help us handle the situation in the best possible way. For example, if we are due for a dose of anxiety, the next potential anxiety-inducing event will be interpreted as such, and our stress fix will be delivered in a tall glass. However, if we are relaxed and not in need of a dramatic episode, the event will be ignored.

Expectations play a large role in the mechanism the subconscious uses to create the unpleasant situation. As we have seen earlier, the negative source of any problem is in the disparity between the result of an event and our expectation of what that result should have been. I went to the bank, and it was closed. I am annoyed, not because the bank is closed, but because I expected it to be open. When we look behind any bad feeling relating to an event, we will find expectation causing the tension.

But are you justified in being stressed or frustrated? You may be, but I am not sure that this is the question you want to be asking. It's quite easy to find people around you who would support you in feeling bad. In fact, this is probably why some of those people hang around. The subconscious knows to make friends for different reasons, and it always has people around for validating bad feelings—a willing audience for the drama show. After all, now your drama becomes their drama: win-win.

The real question is, would you *want* to be frustrated if you had a choice? I can see reasons to go on vacation or eat ice cream because those are fun things, but being anxious and frustrated? We should be looking at ways not to have those things in our lives.

In some cases, having expectations is the pathway to frustration. But do expectations play any positive role? Where would our kids be if we didn't expect anything from them? Where would we be at work if our boss didn't expect anything from us? "I have high expectations of myself" is a statement often made by successful people.

Having high expectations synonymous with success. It seems that we cannot succeed without expecting something from ourselves or having someone else expect something from us.

That may be true. To have success, you have to have expectation. Instead of living with expectation because it is the only way to achieve success, I prefer to question the entire institution of success.

Let's look at what success means. It means a sense of accomplishment. This sense of achieving something grand is genuine and feels good. It has no downside that I can imagine. The question is: Can we have a sense of accomplishment without being successful? The answer is *yes*, and here's why: success is the measurement of our accomplishments in the eyes of other people—hypothetical people, for the most part.

Here's an example from my personal experience. I used to find it very difficult to be able not to do anything. Any time I attempted to do nothing, my mind raced to find some fun activity and coerced me into doing it. When I did manage to have a relaxing time doing nothing, I felt a sense of great accomplishment. However, this accomplishment can't be characterized as a success, since I didn't achieve anything most people would find valuable. The result was not meaningful to anyone else but me. I didn't fail, but I also didn't really succeed.

Success, remember, also has a twin brother, attached at the hip and always there: failure. Remember him? How many endeavors were not attempted by people because of fear of failure? How many were victims of self-sabotage due to it's alter-ego: fear of success?

Failure, in turn, also has some tricks of its own. Ever felt disappointed? Disappointment is not a result of an event. It is the result of an event not going as planned. It is the direct result of having specific expectations and having those expectations not met.

It is supremely important to determine whether your need to succeed comes from an internal desire to feel accomplishment and self-satisfaction or whether it comes from a need to satisfy someone else's standards, be it a parent, a teacher, society at large, or your own ego. Growing up in a family that expects a lot from you can have a long-lasting effect in adulthood where you constantly look for the hypothetical person to satisfy instead of yourself. It can be very difficult later on to find what it is you find to be an accomplishment and pursue it for your own personal satisfaction. In a way, at some point you'll have to decide whether you're looking to succeed or looking to be happy.

Since success, failure, and expectation have so much baggage attached to them, why don't we just do away with the entire thing? Can we deem these ideas unnecessary and just ditch them? Some concepts are such an integral part of our reality that we never question them. Well, let's question them right now, starting with *success*.

Instead of telling you what I think you should do, which I don't care to do so much, I'll share what I have done in my own life, including how I question and eliminate aspects of my reality that I deem pointless and pain-inducing.

QUESTIONING SUCCESS AND FAILURE

Can you imagine living in a reality without success and failure? Is it even possible? Would it be, say, like living in a reality without smiles, crying, or feeling? Can one person decide that a concept playing such a big part in society's reality no longer plays a part in their individual reality?

Yes, and it's sort of fun, too.

The ideas of success, failure, and expectations are no longer a part of my life and haven't been for a while. It's much like how people in Egypt don't contemplate snowfall, and tribesmen in the Amazon don't bother with economic downturns.

It started with analyzing and understanding that the ideas of expectations, success, and failure were contrived and unnecessary. If I can be happy with the result of my efforts, enjoy the fruit of my labor, and feel satisfied with what I do, why label it? Why give it a thumbs-up or thumbs-down sticker that will make it into either a good thing or a bad thing? In my life, everything is always good. I am not saying that I always feel good. I sometimes feel bad, but this is a part of my life, and in the grand scheme of things, I know that feeling bad is not actually a bad thing.

So without the ability to be successful, what drives me? What makes me get up in the morning and do things? Believe it or not, I can't answer that. I get up, put something on, have a cup of Joe, and get to whatever it is I am doing. Since I'm no longer under any delusion that I control what I do, I also don't try to explain it.

It would be like trying to explain why a dog howls at the moon. Pointless.

TRYING

While nixing societal conventions, the next victim is the institution of trying. My new motto is *if you are trying, then you are trying too hard.* But how can one achieve anything without trying? Simple: by doing.

Remember, when we try, we must have an expectation that defines what the result of our efforts will look like. Oops, *expectation* is no longer something I do. Also, when we try, we can either fail or succeed, which are also things I no longer deal with.

I am happy to report that after two years of living *try-free* I have become financially independent. The lack of trying has given me the space to trust that everything will work out as it should. All I did was paint the picture and stopped trying. I let go of controlling my everyday life. Instead, I just watched it happen. I moved myself from inside my head to a good observation spot just above it. I now enjoy seeing what life brings, seeing how I react to it, experiencing events I am a part of, and just loving life.

It's important to note that *not trying* doesn't mean *not doing.* I do, and I do a lot. However, I abandoned the role of controlling what I do and how I do it. Actually, this is not really a role, but rather a pretend role. Sort of like little Maggie in the opening scene of The Simpsons, sitting in the car next to her mom with a tot steering wheel. She may go through all the motions, push with her feet, steer the wheel, and feel anxious about hitting the curb, but her believing she's in control doesn't get her any closer to what she wants.

I found that attempting to control my life has the opposite effect. We look at that effect throughout the book. When I was younger, I believed that everything I have is the result of things I do (which is not completely untrue), but I also believed that I have to make a concentrated effort to come up with the ideas that will bring me what I want and then work hard to implement them. I would get up in the morning and force myself to do. Think, plan, design, sketch. I came up with enough business ideas to fill a library, and the house was plastered with plans for websites, programs, furniture, businesses, and just plain thoughts. Believing that my success would come from sheer effort brought me frustration and anxiety.

These days I rarely get anxious. I am in the flow, feeling good and excited to see what the day will bring. Obviously, I am also writing this book. I started writing it about four years ago. I had an entire outline drawn out, started filling it out, and gave up. Two years later I picked it up again, wrote about eighty-five pages, and as I kept on writing, I realized that the first seventy-five pages were just nonsense. This was a good way for me to figure out my thoughts and get a better understanding of the subject matter, and mainly, that I didn't yet know how to write a book about it.

For a while, I had the typical "I should finish writing that book" thoughts. Then, as a part of my *no-trying philosophy*, I decided that when I am ready for writing this book, I would just get to it without trying.

A few weeks ago, I was sitting with my laptop at a cafe, writing. I looked at my computer and realized that I was writing this book. I could not believe it—I was writing it without even knowing it. Looking at the number of pages I had written, I realized that I had been writing it for at least two or three days. When it was right, it just happened.

Back to trying. We hear many progressive voices tell us that if we want to succeed we have to be willing to fail, but most important, we have to keep trying. What I say is, simply do away with the whole institution of trying and everything that goes with it. This includes failure, success, expectations, and disappointment.

All those heavy concepts can be replaced with simpler things: simply be, and when you feel the urge to do, then do!

Okay, this wasn't fair at all. I went through years of struggle and frustration to figure all this out, and all I have to say to you is "just be?" It's as if I am setting you up for failure. "Sure, just be. You have no idea how to, but really, it's so easy."

Well, it's not, and I don't intend to leave you hanging. There will be chapters later on that give specific instructions and exercises on *how to* get there. I never forget or take for granted the tough steps I had to take to get here.

A MATTER OF SEMANTICS

Isn't it all just how you say it? Are the words success, failure, accomplishment, and satisfaction just different ways of saying the same things?

Not really. These are words that have strong emotional connections to things we experience. They have connections to how we see the world, how we assess reality, and when we feel good or bad. Analyzing various concepts as we just did is very powerful, and the words we use to describe them serve an important purpose.

CHAPTER 9

Emotions

Nothing else tells the story of our lives more accurately than emotions. We live our lives through feeling, and evaluate our days by how we feel. You can ask a person a hundred questions about their situation, but at the end, just asking, "Yes, but how do you feel about it?" can give you the real picture. Being happy, content, or joyful is a condition that surpasses all other reality checks. You can have no money, live alone, have a grinding job, or have anything else that may appear as a bad situation, but if you feel happy a lot of the time, then, well, all is well.

Unfortunately, the current state of the human condition is focused much more on negative emotions. If it weren't, we would not have such high rate of disease, war, and general dissatisfaction. People wouldn't be complaining so much.

But to view emotions as one of several methods for evaluating life events is to miss the big picture. Life is tied to our emotions. Emotions are not another method used to evaluate life. Instead, our emotions are the primary, overriding measure of life's quality. A happy life, or a life where one goes through feeling happy and content, is a good life. You can't say that about any other factor. Money? Marriage? Job? Success? You can find many people who achieved these milestones and are still miserable. I have yet to meet a miserable happy person.

What more do we need in life than to feel good? Not much. The issue we have is that we don't question what society is telling us that we need to be happy. Even worse, society has such well-defined conventions for when we feel good and mostly, when we feel bad, that we don't take the time to figure out if those conventions apply to us. We train ourselves from a young age by mimicking grown-ups to feel bad in specific situations. We put our own signature on our reactions, which make us think that our problems are special and deep, but for the most part, they follow the same conventions as everyone else.

EMOTIONS ARE EFFECT AND CAUSE

Emotions are not just the result of events in our lives—they are why the events happen.

Emotional patterns, or emotional habits, are the driving force behind events in your life and behind your reaction to events. Your emotional reaction to an event colors it either *bad* or *good*. Imagine being stuck in traffic, for example. For many, this can be the trigger for a horrible day or at least a ruined morning. But for some, being stuck in traffic means more alone time to listen to the radio, catch a book on tape, or just chill. So is being in traffic good or bad? It's neither. Your reaction to it makes it *feel* either good or bad, which in turn can be called good or bad. The question, "How was your ride this morning?" can be answered with either,

"Great! Thanks to road construction delays, I had extra time to catch up on the news" or "Horrible! I was in traffic for an hour!"

It is important to understand that there's no way to avoid emotions; they just show up! The emotions we feel are part of a pattern that took a long time to evolve. This doesn't mean, however, that this pattern has to take a long time to be changed. This is because our reactions constantly revamp our mood patterns. Let us spend a moment to see how this works.

The mechanism that makes us react emotionally has no imagination. Instead, it is trying to match its earlier experience. It is much like owning a dog. If you neglected to train it, it'll do what it wants. You'll then think that the dog does what it wants, and you'll be right. While it will be the truth, it is mostly because, as its owner, you never corrected its instinctive reactions.

But at which point can you start? Every time the dog misbehaves, you have a chance to correct its behavior. This means that chances to fix what you created are endless. The same thing is true with our emotions. Our chance to make a change appears every time we have a negative emotional reaction.

JUSTIFIED EMOTIONS

Aren't some emotional reactions justified? Do we have to turn into emotionally controlled drones that always react properly? Of course not!

Being emotional is okay as long as it doesn't wreak havoc in our lives on a regular basis or make us plain miserable. The goal is to observe our emotions in specific situations. Watch during the week and see what type of event is the consistent trigger for a strong negative emotional reaction. Want a quick way to get that done? Ask someone you live with—your spouse, kids (beware—they tend to be brutally honest), a friend, or a co-worker. Even though you may not be aware, they are all very much aware of what puts you in a bad mood. This may be a huge blind spot for you (as it is for many other people), but others in your life see it and probably discuss it on occasion. If you do ask, brace yourself for something you most likely will not like to hear.

Pay attention to those recurring responses. Think about it: Why even have those reactions if you're not there to enjoy them? You can sometimes take great joy at feeling miserable. A good cry, some self-pity, and some attention from someone can be a lot of fun. The events I'm talking about, however, are unconscious reactions that make you and people around you unhappy. You would do well to recognize them, observe them, and possibly later on even have them almost stop altogether.

Not all moods are caused by opportunist reactions to random events. Some of mood episodes are orchestrated by our subconscious to bring on the right emotion at the right time.

Our emotions are not random and are not the result of random events. Instead, they are on a schedule. Much like any other physiological or psychological need we have such as eating, sleeping, smoking, taking a leak, playing Xbox, etc., our negative emotions build a need that has to be fulfilled. In a case where there is no proper opportunity for the specific emotion to express itself, we will create a situation that will give us the excuse to feel the way we need to feel.

While emotions are such a big part of our everyday lives, we seem to be clueless about how to make them our own. We fail miserably at understanding the importance our feelings have on our lives today and how we can work with them to melt away painful habits and create a better-feeling future.

EMOTIONS AS A DESIGN TOOL

Imagining how life would be is only a part of the creation process. If visualization is the light bulb, then emotions are the electricity. If positive thinking is a car, then feeling strong emotions are the gas and brake pedals. Yes, you guessed it: positive emotions are the gas, and negative emotions are the brakes.

Let's say that you want to find a new, well-paying job where you can be creative and spend your day doing what you like. You might be able to make it happen through visualization and intention. So you go on a reality road trip, destination: new job. As you sit at the wheel making this happen, the positive emotions you place behind your intention will make you move toward your goal. If the overwhelming feelings you have are flavored with "it will never happen," "I'm not good enough," or "it's impossible to make money doing what you love," then the positive ideas behind your intention will never be able to push you forward.

Letting go of the anxiety and propelling yourself with *intensely positive feelings* will push you forward. The energetic impression positive emotions add to a goal you set is the matter from which your desired reality is made. It never runs out and doesn't cost any money.

CONSEQUENCES OF THOUGHTS AND ACTIONS

Like it or not, life is a closed loop: what we do to the outside of our lives affects our own reality to the same degree and in the same way. The flavor of what we get from life is the flavor we put out; there are no exceptions to that rule.

There are many sayings that describe that phenomenon, such as "you reap what you sow," "you've made your bed, now lie in it," and many more. All those are in some way scientifically accurate.

When we act, speak, and feel, we emit wave energy. It is sometimes referred to as Karma or vibes. When we express something, besides our voices, words, body language, and facial expressions, we also emit those vibes. The vibe energy is imprinted with whatever it is we are expressing. It is affecting the subject we're relating to and is directed at other people in the room as well as on ourselves. You also added that energy to the world, making it a tiny-bit more like the energy you emitted. Remember we spoke earlier about how you are doing much more good in the world when you're happy? This is a big part of it. All our combined vibes fill the world and affect it.

But in context to this book, there's no such thing as doing to others without it being done to you. As you do it to anyone else, at the same time, you're sending an encoded request to the universe to get you the same sentiment in a yet unknown package.

These thoughts also make us question the true impact of revenge. When we take any action in retribution to something that was done to us, we're achieving quite the opposite.

CHAPTER 10

More about Our Human Condition

MORE EGO GAMES

Remember the ego, your conjoined twin? Well, it has another really annoying habit we need to discuss. As soon as you become good at something or move up in some way, it likes to take credit. It also likes to start pointing out how much better you are than anyone else is.

We need to watch this opportunist trait closely, because the minute we start to identify ourselves as "being good at something," we get out of the flow, and our ability to perform drops.

It can be difficult to notice the switch because it feels so good to take credit for a job well done. The telltale sign of the switch is that we start to compare ourselves to others who don't yet see what we see or who are not as good at something as we are.

For example, if you became a vegetarian, you may start to feel superior to people that still eat meat. If you are good at a certain sport and move up in the ranks, you may start to feel a sense of entitlement.

We may want to realize that being in the flow brought us to where we are—not believing that we were better than anyone else was. As long as we enjoy comparing ourselves to people who are not at our level or who don't have our point of view, our ability to perform at that level is going to be compromised, and our level of enjoyment from that particular activity is eventually going to drop.

Enjoying being good at something is a great feeling. As humans, we hold it one of our most precious life goals. We live to find out what we love to do, do it, and discover just how high we can push ourselves. Once the joy shifts from doing and achieving to feeling that we're somehow better than anyone else, the overall experience is going to suffer, our performance is going to drop, and we are going backward instead of forward.

Personally, I noticed that kind of shift when I started running. I realized I could run much longer distances than I imagined. Shortly after starting to run, I kicked off my shoes and ran barefoot: first a few miles, then a few half marathons. It didn't take long for me to start feeling that I was better because I didn't run with shoes, and I was certainly better than those 5K runners were. Why would I want to run 5K when I can run a half marathon?

Shortly after that, I realized just how stupid my thoughts sounded. This self-pat on the back turned into sort of a joke whenever I caught myself basking in my so-called greatness.

Soon after, my ego realized that I was not going to identify myself as a runner by comparing myself to anyone else. Those thoughts became less frequent, and my ability to run steadily increased. Instead of being a "proud barefoot runner," I got back to being a person who happened to sometimes run barefoot.

FOMO

FOMO is a great term that refers to one of my favorite social disorders: Fear of Missing Out. We have all felt FOMO before. Something fun is happening somewhere, and we were not included. Experiencing that sort of anxiety regularly can point to a tool used by the subconscious to distract us from what matters, which is where we are right now, not what we could be doing. What matters most is being present and content.

It is important to realize that the ego creates the anxiety that we may be missing out on something. Theoretically, we could always be doing something else more fun than what we are doing. The key is knowing that we cannot be doing anything other than what we are doing at any given time. When there is another fitting opportunity, it will make itself known in good time. Being anxious will only cloud our ability to recognize opportunities.

So what to do? After all, when anxiety takes hold, it doesn't exactly ask for permission.

The first step is to affirm that you realize, intellectually, that your best bet for taking advantage of opportunities is to be confident and in the moment. When we're in the flow, opportunities knock on our doors just as we are ready for them. Forcing opportunities makes less-than-good experiences.

The easy thing about handling such situations is answering the magic question: Is there anything I can or am willing to do about it right now? It is usually negative. Usually feeling left out leaves us with a crappy, helpless feeling with no course of action. Like many other situations, when we have no course of action, the thing to do is to let go. Drop it. Forget about it on the spot. You heard that so-and-so is having a party, but you haven't been invited. Well, either get on the phone and get yourself invited or don't. Either way, you'll have to drop the subject afterward. Every time you feel obsessed with it, just say, "If it's a good thing for me to be there, I'll be there."

Not being included can be a great thing. I remember when a friend of ours in the neighborhood had a big garden party, and we weren't invited. This was hurtful at the start, but then we realized that this friendship was built on control and social games we weren't interested in playing. We cooled that relationship, reevaluated our approach to friendships, and a whole new part of our lives opened up in front of us. Instead of obsessing about being left out and missing a social event, we turned it into a positive turning point.

FOMO also applies to life on a grand scale. There are always going to be infinitely more things we have not experienced than the ones we did. Missed opportunities, regretful decisions, what-ifs, and I-could've-been thoughts can haunt us if we let them. The first thing we have to do, right now, is agree that spending any energy lamenting things we can't have back is debilitating and has a negative impact on our ability to do positive things in the future.

Did feeling helpless and regretful ever do anything good for you? Did it ever propel you to new heights? I doubt it. Right now, say to yourself, "I can only reverse my course and make positive things happen in my life if I let go of obsessing about what did or didn't happen in the past."

Once that initial understanding starts to seep in, a mental process can start to change. You will slowly learn to catch the unhelpful thoughts before they become full-fledged anxieties. You will still feel what you feel but not identify with it. You will get the thought that says, "Damn, I was not included, again!" But you will be less likely to convert it into frustration and into follow-up thoughts such as, "My life sucks," "No one wants me around," or other thoughts of that kind that don't serve any purpose aligned with your intent. As a result, because you are no longer in a needy state, you will certainly be invited to take part in more activities.

THE AMAZING FORK IN THE ROAD

Let's talk a bit about opportunities for change. We discussed that while it is all up to us, and the ability to change our lives is within reach, it isn't easy to do and takes time.

We also discussed the circular nature of how reality is created. We start with our beliefs, and the subconscious uses our beliefs to form our reality. Next, we observe that self-painted reality, and our beliefs that this is indeed how reality is become strengthened. From there the loop continues: our newly affirmed beliefs regenerate our reality, and so on.

When we are stuck in a loop that we are looking to change, it is important to know where we can jump out and what we are jumping on to.

The loop of creation can never stop. Belief will always create reality, which in turn will reinforce belief. That's not a good or bad thing; it's just how it is. Our goal is to change our beliefs, and one way to do it is find the opening in the loop and use that opening to make a tweak. That opening is very simply in our reactions.

It can sometimes seem that our reactions are an objective form of expression that mimics what we see. We hear a joke, we laugh; we see a sad movie, we tear up; something frustrating happens, and we get annoyed. Ooh...hold on right there! We need to pay close attention to these negative reactions.

The real opening for change in life's loop is in events that cause us to feel bad in some way. That slim opening in the loop, that elusive fraction of a second that can change our lives, fits snugly between an event and our reaction to it.

At first, we can only observe our reactions to these events. Our reactions are still too automatic and can't be stopped. Before we know it, we're already annoyed, anxious, pissed, stressed, sad, or telling the whole story to someone in a manner reminiscent of complaining.

But as these events happen, and we react to them, we can slowly start to wake up in the middle of the negative experience and observe it. Observe the event, and observe your reactions, even after it has already happened. Realize that the entire event was scripted to get a reaction from you and to get you to feel the way you feel. Knowing that and keeping it in your mind while you feel bad about something sort of takes the edge off. It allows you to get closer and closer to a point where the initial negative reaction is interrupted with a sliver of awareness. This sliver expands and eventually can turn into a fully formed thought, such as "It is happening. I am reacting negatively to an event."

Our ability to intercept those incidents where negative emotions are triggered, and separate our reactions from the event can have sweeping implications. If our reactions can actually become our own reactions rather than a habitual response, eventually those automatic reactions will be replaced with the new set of reactions, and a new, positive cycle will be created.

FEELING BAD

Again, we may think, "Feeling bad is a part of life. Why would I want to not feel what I feel?" This is a good point, and it has two answers.

First, we should always feel what we feel! If you feel bad, don't jump around trying to rid yourself of the feeling. Be inside of it. Feel it all the way. When you feel a certain way, it is too late not to feel that way.

With all that, wouldn't you want to feel good instead? Wouldn't you want to have things that made you feel bad before not affect you in that way? We sometimes identify with the bad feelings we have. They are romantic, tragic, and can make us feel alive. However, when the romantic part wears out and only pain and emptiness remain, it is not all that fun. Remember, pain is at the end of every drama. If you choose to accept this pain and see nothing wrong with it, I have nothing to add. These reactions have other implications that make your life less than ideal. Negative aspects of our life situation are all connected. It is impossible to live peacefully with only one side of negativity in our lives—negativity tends to like company.

THE FORK

So, where is the fork in the road? The fork in the road is a decision we have to make. We have to choose between the old comfortable, automatic way and going in a bold, new direction. This decision will be laid in front of us every time we catch our egos taking over and every time we have negative feelings. I am not suggesting that you not feel bad. As I said before, feeling bad is a fact as soon as it happens, so be in it. But at the same time, know that it is an automatic reaction. Know that there need not be a continuation of the bad feelings beyond the first burst. There's no need to identify with the message the negative emotions send. The message with the feeling is always stinging: What if I run out of money? What if I'm a bad mom? What if I am fired? I am so mad at so-and-so.

One side of the fork is choosing the old way through identification, where we believe the message the ego sends. This choice will lead us right back to where we started and ensure that the cycle of negativity, and all the pain that is inherent in it, lives on.

The other side of the fork is to choose a new direction: allowing ourselves to feel bad but letting the message go. A person choosing this path might think, "I feel bad, and I have the urge to blame someone, but I know that I feel bad just because, well, because I feel bad. This time I won't take it out on anyone, including myself." Or, "I feel bad, but I know that my life is going to turn out just fine. I'll have enough money to pay the rent even if right now I don't really know where it's coming from. These negative thoughts are a habit, and I am letting them go."

RESISTANCE

To be in the flow, we have to understand that the flow is made of constant motion. Healthy, happy, energetic motion. Being in the flow means only allowing and never resisting.

This concept can be a bit tricky at first. After all, we don't want many things in life. Are we supposed to allow them to be? Well, it's not that simple. The resistance I am talking about is inner resistance. It's resistance to ideas, how we feel, and everything that is. Resistance is so instinctive that it appears to be the only way we can react.

Eventually, after we are in the flow long enough, there will be nothing to resist. There may be actions that may appear to be resisting something to an outside observer, but there will not be any sense of resistance in you.

Instead of resisting, we can let go. We are constantly being presented with encouragement from our egos to hold onto things, which is actually resisting letting go. We can choose to stop resisting and let go of them.

The inner resistance we have is manifested through subconscious reactions. We see something happen or encounter a situation, and, like a condescending grown-up, the ego goes, "Oh, no. No, no, no!" The grip the resistance has on us is swift and all encompassing. It leaves very little room for illumination, and light would allow us to be present and evaluate our actions. Seeing through that instant resistance takes practice and forethought. It takes thinking about the big picture at a time where the subconscious has us convinced that the only course of action is to control the situation and resist the natural flow of things.

In a way, since resistance is the opposite of the flow, finding resistance and treating it is most important. The first step is realizing resistance exists internally and is responsible for the pain in our lives. It is responsible for keeping us out of the flow.

Next, we set up an internal alarm to go off when we resist anything. This can be interesting. Resistance is so fundamentally built-in to our reactions that pulling it out and pointing at it takes practice.

The third step is to let go. Let go. Let go, and then let go some more. Some days I walk around the entire day just telling myself repeatedly: *Let go. Just let go.*

Let go.

OUR GENIUS

Regardless of what they stuck in your head during middle school, genius is not that kid with glasses who was good at math. Genius is found, in a very real and practical way, in every one of us. Our genius light shines when we find our purpose and live in line with it.

By purpose, I don't mean some grand, world-altering plan the universe has for you where you will find yourself leading the masses to salvation. Your purpose, or your brilliance, can be something much simpler and close to earth. You know what it is, because regardless of what your parents really wanted you to be, what drives you nuts is *that* one thing. It can be working with animals, cooking, growing things, cutting hair, making people laugh, painting, healing people or animals, teaching, playing tennis, or anything else people do on this planet. No matter what it is, we were each imprinted with a general direction, and the more we are in line with that direction, the more we are in the flow and the happier we are.

When we find and follow that direction, or find what we can do that is in line with our innate passion, we can fully express our potential. Furthermore, once we tap this potential and follow it, our lives become surprisingly much easier. Things just seem to happen without trying. We are in the flow.

Once you give up the idea that there's a difference between having fun and making a living, and you couple that with following your passion, the world starts to seem like a really fun place to be.

Not teaching this is, in my judgment, a big injustice schools do to children. Schools start out by stripping any thoughts kids have that what they want to do or like to do matters. Kids are left to follow some arbitrary, boring, generic track and are told that they can't make a living doing what they love.

Let me tell you: you can make a living at what you love to do, and when you do, your life's "fun-to-problems ratio" will gradually shift in the direction of fun.

On top of that, you will be helping others. No matter what you do, by following this innate talent and attraction you have toward a certain field, you'll live a happier life and affect those around you positively.

But due to the government-sanctioned brainwashing kids get in school, many go out to the world having no idea what they want to be or what they love to do. They go to college to get some degree, hoping something clicks, or they pick a profession based on the earning potential of this field or another.

No matter where we are in life, and no matter how deeply our passions have been buried, it is up to each one of us to go and find it. Spending time doing what we were meant to be doing is an experience we owe to ourselves. Go find it.

WE ARE SPECIAL

The question is, if everyone's a genius, aren't we just all ordinary? How can I be special if everyone is special?

The need to compare ourselves to others and determine our value by the comparison is messy. No matter what we do, there will always be someone who is considered better and many who are worse.

The ego's realm is to compare people, assign a value to each one, and rank itself in comparison.

We would do well to evaluate how much we focus on comparing ourselves to others because the other end of it is always painful. The more we identify with being better than someone else, and the more that thought boosts us emotionally, the worse the fall will be at the end.

Each one of us can be special, and even though we all are special, everyone we meet can appreciate and recognize our unique brilliance regardless of how we believe we stack up.

ARE WE MAD?

Of course not. If we were mad, wouldn't we know it? Wouldn't people be either avoiding us or pointing at us in the street? Aren't people who have "lost it" somehow marked? Don't they have bus passes on a string tied around their necks? Of course we are not mad, you and I.

But wait! Isn't one of the known facts about crazy people that they don't know that they are crazy? Yes it is. Crazy people don't know that they are crazy. The subconscious keeps them unaware of their madness. Their ego has taken over many operations, and most of them believe that they are completely sane, like you and I! Ah. Hold on. How do you know you're not crazy? Seriously, how do you know?

Let me help you out: you are, and there's no question about it. In fact, we all are.

If I were to draw a rough, nonscientific scale, where a completely enlightened person has an insanity level of zero, and a person in confinement in a mental institution is ten, everyone you know, including yourself, falls somewhere between four and seven. We are not too crazy, and we are functional for the most part, but we are not by any means sane.

If you paid attention so far, you'll see that I pointed out hundreds of bits of madness that went completely uncontested.

Insanity can be traced back to one unquestionable aspect of our existence: ego. Our egos reign over thoughts and actions in a way that cannot be defined any other way. Imagine a person walking down the street, talking loudly to some nonexistent entity, looking back periodically. He's mad, no doubt. But what about you? A remarkably similar dialog is constantly going on inside your head. The difference between you and the crazy dude is that your insanity hasn't taken that strong a hold of you yet (I assume), and you can still manage to keep it to yourself. However, the ego is still there, planting mad thoughts in your mind. The insanity is not that you have an ego, but rather that the ideas it gives you go unquestioned. If your ego tells you that it's your parents' fault that your life is a mess, you believe it. If it tells you that the only thing to do to live is to take a shot of alcohol, you take it. The ego's insane ideas slowly become habits that are difficult to break.

Tell me, where are you when your ego makes you do all those things? You are unaware. The ego can hide things from us even as we do them. We take actions that we can't be held responsible for. We would lose the weight but for the voice that told us to get that slice of cake. The plea is not guilty; instead, we may be overweight by reason of insanity.

Almost every part of this book points out aspects of our insanity. The things we do may not appear to be crazy because they are common, but they are insane.

The sane thing to do is to observe and let go. Observe yourself thinking. Observe how thoughts come to your mind, fill you with emotions, and call for action.

This observation is sanity. It slowly melts away insanity as a person once more becomes aware and witnesses the ego do things that it is used to doing when it's not observed.

CHAPTER 11

Goals

While we all know that goals are essential to achieving anything we want in life, we don't always know how to make them work for us. It seems like a no-brainer: set a goal and then work to achieve it. The goal is there to remind us why we want to achieve it, and we take actions that are supposed to make our goals happen.

If it were that easy, more goals would have been reached, and there would be much less frustration and self-doubt. The fact is, setting and reaching goals doesn't work quite that way because We are using the conscious mind to do work that it wasn't intended to do. How could we possibly know what to do to achieve our goals? There are just so many variables involved that trying to analyze them all and take actions based on our own consideration is like trying to balance the United States budget with a calculator.

Yes, I know people do set goals and succeed; however, they don't succeed due to trying hard enough. They succeed *despite* trying.

WHAT ABOUT MOTIVATION?

Motivated people achieve their goals, of course. But while motivation is a necessary tool, if the mental conditions aren't right, our motivation will fall short.

Here's a metaphor that can help. Let's say that our goal is a cloud in the sky, and we're trying to reach our goal. For a while, it seems far and impossible. We have a jet pack we can use to reach our cloud, but it is empty.

Then, we remember all the reasons why we wanted to reach our goal. Those motivational thoughts fill the tank, and we can use the jet pack. We strap it on and fly to the cloud goal. We reached our goal and are happy.

Unfortunately, the jet pack runs out of fuel, gravity pulls us back, and we find ourselves back on earth, away from our goal. Motivation, much like a jet pack, has the intensity to get us places but not to keep us there. Staying at a goal requires being on the same plane as it is. It requires that beliefs align with the goal.

Working on changing our beliefs achieves this. We can slowly change those beliefs until they become more aligned with our goal.

This scenario explains why achieving goals is mostly a temporary thing. People are motivated, they expand energy, and they overcome the subconscious to change how they look, their material status, their social scene, or their addiction. But unless the core beliefs have been changed as well, the subconscious will prevail in undoing the amazing work done to reach the goal, and it will revert the person back to his or her old self.

HOW GOALS SHOULD BE APPROACHED

To achieve goals, action is not all we need. In fact, actions will be taking themselves. What we have to do is work on how we think and what we believe. To make things happen, we have to separate our efforts into three parts:

1. *Paint a picture with feeling. Imagine the joy of the goal, as if it has been achieved.*
2. *Allow. Let go of controlling how or when the goal will be materialized.*
3. *Act blindly. Take steps as they are unveiled to allow the goal to manifest.*

Do you see any trying there? Struggle? Hard work? Pondering thousands of possible actions and billions of potential results? Nope. All of those things are blockers.

What you do see is allowing and letting go of control. It means trusting rather than stressing, and it means enjoying the moment rather than struggling with details.

The accepted form of setting goals can backfire quickly and cause you disappointment and discouragement. To understand that, let us look at a typical example. You're dancing to an aerobic video, and the instructor urges you to imagine your goal and think about how happy you will be when you achieve it. This sounds like a good idea, but the reality is that the ego will be expecting results in the physical mirror in hours or days, and results are not going to be there for weeks or months. This disparity between expectation and what you perceive reality to be is certain to cause frustration and disappointment. The part of us that deals with expectations has a very short attention span and gets discouraged quickly if left hanging too long. Telling it, "Hey, we're going to be fit" and then expecting it to wait for three months to see any difference whatsoever just doesn't work. We have to think of a strategy for setting goals without creating that gap between *what is* and *what we want*.

It's important to know how to separate doing from setting goals. Different parts of us set and reach goals, and they should not mix. We perform the first part—including goal setting, visualization, and internalization. We consciously see things as we want them to be. This can't be done automatically, like other things in our lives.

The other part is the actual work. We don't control this part, but the subconscious handles it. All we have to do is show up and not interrupt. Watch your lips move, listen to words come out, watch yourself make phone calls, buy things you need for your goal, fix up the space you need, and start working. All that happens as if you're having an out-of-body experience. Your arms move, your hands grab onto things, action is taken, and all you have to do is smile.

SETTING GOALS

Proper goal setting is a joyful and powerful mental process of creation. We can visualize the future, but at the same time, we are fully in the moment.

The goal you imagine should be as close as possible to what you really want: to feel good! A girlfriend is a way to feel good (if you're single and into girls, of course), as is a successful career. This means that your goal should be thought about and imagined but also very much felt. Experience your goal as if it has already been achieved and with waves of joyful emotions.

There are three preferred methods of internalizing goals: feeling, seeing, or hearing. Some people, when imagining their goal, find it more convincing to see it happen in the mind rather than feeling it, and some prefer to imagine hearing it.

Let's try it. Think about a goal right now. Don't make it crazy, but put it right outside the borders of your comfort zone. Now, imagine yourself after you achieved your goal. Imagine how happy you'd be, knowing that what seemed impossible in the past is now reality. Feel how grateful you are to the people and events that helped you along the way, and ponder the amazing coincidences that helped you get there. If you want an object, imagine the joy of looking at it. No doubts—this is your internal mind dreaming, and there are no boundaries.

Now, how did that feel? If it felt good, you just demonstrated that you are able to create! If it was confusing, embarrassing, or unnatural, you may need to get over yourself and practice a bit more.

Putting an intense, positive emotional energy behind our goals unleashes an incredible power of creation. This is not something that we were taught as kids so it can be difficult to grasp as grown-ups. The part that we call *planning* gets credit for aiding in the actual creation. It is exactly the other way. Seeing the desired result and putting emotion behind it is the creative process. Being creative does not mean being able to pointlessly imagine things. When we use our creativity to imagine anything, we are, in fact, creating. What comes after is the physical manifestation of what is already created in the quantum field. That, and a lot of letting go of resistance. I urge you to take this to heart even if it is simply for the sake of an exercise.

GOAL-SETTING BLOCKERS

While setting and fine-tuning our desires, there can be no concern as to how they will actually come to be. For a goal to be registered with the subconscious, the universe, and everything else that will push it along, we need to be in the flow. There can be no doubt or anxiety about our chances to make it happen for two reasons: (1) any negativity while setting goals is a blocker, and (2) you don't have to be concerned with the details since you're not the one who's going to manifest your goal.

It may seem impossible to imagine a big goal without doubts creeping in or the need to dive into the details and try to force yourself to see the things that are not yet on the horizon. If you want to retire early, be fit, find someone amazing to be with, buy an expensive car, or what have you, if you have never done it before, how can you possibly know how to do it? Doubts, anxiety, and micromanaging thoughts will interrupt you, and there's nothing you can do about it. But how you react to those thoughts is up to you.

There are two options here, so let's draw them up with a little example. You decide to set a goal to own a Porsche. You imagine yourself with the car when a thought creeps in: those cars are unreasonably expensive and unrealistic.

This thought is not right, wrong, correct, or real, and it is not giving you sound advice. If owning a Porsche is what you desire, then it is doable, realistic, and a good thing! The challenge is to let go, but it can be tough. You automatically identify with a thought because it seems as if you came up with it and that it is the reality.

Your choice now is to follow one of these two options:

1. Identify with the thought: "Yeah, I guess this was too much for me. I need to be more realistic and not try to reach so high."

2. Stick by your goal: "Thank you for the warning, but manifesting a Porsche is what I intend to do, and I feel perfectly fine about it."

Now, of course, it could be that at this point in your life, it just doesn't fit to own a Porsche. That is an entirely different issue. You can have the things you were meant to have. When you believe you can do it and fuel that belief with your newly found creative power, the sky is the limit.

PRACTICE VISUALIZATION

Setting a goal is not a one-time thing. You have to go back to it and experience the joy of achieving your goal repeatedly. Every time you think about it, simply stop, close your eyes, and intensely feel how good it is to have what you're looking to manifest. Every time you do, you put more creative energy behind it and reiterate your intention to your subconscious.

It's a bit like training a dog. Repetition is key.

LETTING GO

The next step is possibly the most difficult: trust that the subconscious is a million times more capable that the conscious mind and that trying to control the manifestation process will only hinder it.

In short, get out of the way. The subconscious will tell you what to do, as certain actions are needed. Whenever I set a goal and work to manifest it, I sometimes become anxious about the progress or have the feeling that I need to "do something," "plan something," or just move it forward in some way. It's natural to want to push things along, but doing it in a forced way will not have any positive result. It might make me feel like I'm helping, but I know I'm not.

What I do in those cases is two things:

1. I let go. I tell myself that I trust that when something I will need to do to push things along is the right thing, I will just be doing it, not thinking, "I should do this or that."

2. When I feel like I need to advance things along, I take a minute to reiterate my intention. I close my eyes and positively picture myself after I achieved my goal. I imagine how good it feels to be there and how grateful I am to have what I have. I carry this feeling intensely for a minute or two, if that, and then I forget about it.

I don't need to push for anything more. I have learned to trust that my subconscious will either get me where I want to be, using me to do the work, or will block me if I try to push forward. I learned to enjoy seeing myself take action while it seems like the action is actually taking me. For example, I am sitting here right now writing this. I don't really control what I am writing; it just sort of comes out. If I had to sit myself down and force myself to figure out which word combination would make the biggest impact and bring the most benefit to the reader, I would end up with a very contrived, three-page book, in about five years. Compared to my subconscious, I am like a single-cell organism trying to ride a bicycle. I don't get on a plane and barge into the cockpit demanding to fly it myself. Instead, I trust the crew to get me where I need to go. I also don't go to a restaurant asking to cook the dinner myself. I trust the chef to present me with a perfect meal.

The subconscious is a miracle machine that can make anything we desire happen as long as we trust it and allow it. Then go ahead, desire! Do it often, with intensity and while feeling good. And then, let go; there are forces within us that can carry our requests and convert them into an atom-based objects and events in our lives.

IN THE MOMENT, IN THE FUTURE

We know that being in the moment puts us in the flow, but how can we be in the moment when we're imagining how things will be in the future? Isn't imagining ourselves after we achieve our goals the same as living in the future?

It can be. If the focus is "things are okay now, but they will be great later," the focus is on the future, and the subtext is "things are not as good now." We can be in the present while imagining the future when we focus on how good it feels right now to imagine what we will have. We can experience that intense feeling of achievement right now without considering the "realistic" view that those things are not manifested and that we really have no idea how to make them happen.

We can be fully in the moment, remembering an event in our past or creating a future event in our minds. When we start having regret about the past or anxiety about the future, we start to be stuck and are no longer in the flow.

THIS CAN'T FAIL

The meaning is not that you will definitely get what you want. It means that entering into the world of manifestation with any anxiety that "If it doesn't work out, it will be a failure" is a bad idea. When you rely on the concept of success and failure to determine how you feel about your progress, you automatically block your progress. You are doing this for you—no one else is sitting with a stopwatch to see if you can break your own manifestation record. No one is looking at you, making sure you visualize correctly. No one else has a meaningful interest in you achieving your goal other than you. Your interest, however, is to feel good, so feel good! Thoughts like, "What if I don't manage to get what I set out to get?" will haunt you to some degree, but that's not totally a bad thing. Your reaction to them is the key.

You could say, "Thank you for worrying, but since this is for me, as long as I'm in the moment, everything is just right!" The less you identify with success and failure thoughts, the weaker and more seldom they will become.

MYSTERIOUS WAYS, SURPRISING MEANS

While our goal may be just to be happy, we have to have some idea what we want. We have to let go of knowing how it will come to us. When we focus on how, we are constraining the subconscious ability to make things happen for us. We trust the subconscious because it has resources far beyond our understanding. The subconscious is plugged right into the zero-point field, the Internet of the universe, and the brain of life itself. Let it do its work and don't question or guess the means in which the package will be delivered. The whole point is that from where we stand, we probably can't see the event that will start the ball rolling and put us where we want to be. If we did see it, we'd be already there.

As an example, if you wish for a mate, it is probably not going to be the person you have been unsuccessfully chasing after for years. So setting your intention on getting to date that specific person is silly and defeats the purpose. How about this intention: I am dating someone amazing that I love. This way, you open yourself to whichever way your subconscious chooses to deliver that person to your door. It will, and you will go, "Holy cow, I had no idea!" Fun.

SHOWING UP

So by now your intention is set, you let go of trying to control the process, and you let go of doubts and the fear of failure. All you have to do now is be present and listen for queues. Don't resist anything; don't say no to anything. Say yes to everything. You are an actor on the stage of creation. The lines are fed to you as you need to say them, and you marvel at how it is all just falling together.

This whole scenario of letting go and just allowing the subconscious to guide us may seem a bit counter intuitive. After all, aren't we supposed to take charge and drive the process? Yes, but by setting the agenda, being creative in your imagination, and being present as it all comes together. There are things we were meant to do, and there are things we are able to do but do very poorly. You can and should be a part of the creation process. Just know your place. Know what form your involvement should take and stick to it.

EXPLAINING YOUR GOAL

Another method you may find useful is simply to speak directly to the powers within you to explain your goal and your desire to accomplish it.

It is easier to avoid negative thoughts while you emphatically describe what you want. Of course, that does involve talking to yourself aloud, so if you have an issue with that, either get over it or just don't do it.

Personally, my problem with talking to myself is that I tend to do it when other people are around—unintentionally, of course. My wife will often ask me to whom I am talking, so I'll explain the whole conversation and then get back to it.

The shower is a great place to have conversations with people, and they have no idea that I am naked!

This method of talking to your subconscious or ego (or whatever) worked great for me when about a year ago I wanted to get back to working out. As many others do, I have a horrible time getting back into it after some time off. What I did is firmly explain to my subconscious that while I have no chance to go against it in a battle of wills, I happen to be the one that is setting the agenda around here. I told it that while procrastination was a habit I got it used to and tolerated, it is no longer going to be acceptable. Further, I told it that not only will it no longer stand in my way; it is now responsible to be on alert. Whenever the thought of going to run passes through my head, it is responsible for getting me upstairs to put on my running gear and getting me outside.

It worked like a miracle. In the following weeks, I found myself out running without even remembering how I got there. Once the subconscious is behind us, anything is possible. We think going to work out is difficult (as is anything else we avoid, for that matter), but the reality is that the subconscious works really hard to prevent us from doing what we try to do. For the subconscious, having you put on your gear and go running is just as easy as making you procrastinate and distracting you. Finding an alternate activity and everything that goes along with it is no easy task.

So give it a shot! Explain to yourself and your subconscious, ego, etc. that there are new rules. Explain the new agenda, the goal, and assert your command. Explain in detail what actions you expect and what will no longer be tolerated. This method may be useful and may even be fun.

MAKING YOUR GOAL SUSTAINABLE

Whatever we manage to manifest in life, we should also align our long-term beliefs with it. Even if the manifestation had the intended result, when our deep-rooted core beliefs are not aligned with it, the situation can revert to how it was.

Make sure to focus on writing new beliefs to match at the same time that you work on manifesting things and situations.

Along with this: I am dating someone wonderful.

Add this: I have beautiful, meaningful long-term relationships.

Or along with: I am driving a new car.

Add this: I take care of my property and enjoy it for a long time.

What is the difference between those two affirmations, and why is this important? The first affirmation will get you what you want. The second one will have you keep it.

If you manifested money in your life, you will have money, but you may still lack the ability to be comfortable having it. The result will be that you will soon after lose that money. Holding on to what you have is not at all a given thing. Affirmations for attaining anything must be coupled with affirmations that will make you at peace with having that thing in the long term.

ABOUT MEDITATION

While I believe meditation can be an amazing part of your life, I could never get myself meditate to save my life. The reason I am making this point is that in this age of self-discovery, power of intention, live in the moment, and quantum new brave world, it is easy to believe that nothing good can happen unless you meditate regularly.

This is just plain wrong. Meditation, yoga, Tai Chi, or any other such discipline can be powerful tools. If you use them, they are great, and if you don't, don't think twice about it.

There are many things that if you do them, you may be taking a step back. But there is no single thing you have to do to have a happy life. There are many ways to go about it. If anyone out there believes that meditation is a required ingredient in a peaceful, joyful life, send me a line, and I'll set you straight.

At the same time I'm writing this, I am fully aware that if I did meditate regularly, I could probably experience life in a much deeper way and understand myself, my subconscious, my ego, and the universe on a deeper level. I also believe that a time will come when I will find myself sitting on the floor having just been in deep meditative state, happy and all.

When that day comes, I'll know, because I'll find myself sitting down with my eyes close, focusing on my breath. At this point, meditation is not a priority for me, and I am not losing sleep over it.

If meditation is a priority for you, make sure not to push yourself on it. Instead of resolving to start regular meditation sessions, just to realize the temporary nature of such resolutions, maybe go a different route: imagine yourself as a person who meditate. Your first meditation should be imagining yourself meditating regularly. Do that a few times and it will start to stick. If meditation is a path you were meant to follow, then you will get to be meditating. Forcing ourselves to meditate most likely won't have good results.

WHAT ABOUT PRAYER

The subject of whether prayer works or not is a sort of debate I consider a fantastic waste of time. I can tell you right now, and you can quote me on this: prayer always work, just mostly not how we may expect it to.

What does it mean? Isn't a prayer a personal thing? Is there a right and wrong way to pray?

Yes.

Here's the short version: When you say: "God, I am so poor. Why did you make me so poor? I want more money!" or "God, please, I want to score with that hot chick from Dunkin' Donuts" you are focusing on what you do not have. Your focus is being poor, or your wanting something. In prayer language, you do not get what you ask for, you get what you focus on.

In the first example, the focus was on the not-have, the poor and the frustration. The second prayer was far too specific. What you want is not this girl or boy, what you want is a great girl or boy! One that fits you and will love you. It might end up being that same person, but the focus is on feeling great in a relationship, not the mechanics or checkmark of scoring with someone specific.

The correct way to phrase the same prayers would be:

"God, I am so grateful for everything I have. Thank you for making sure that I always have everything I need just as I need it, and that I never lack anything.", and, "God - thank you for having an amazing girl planned out for me. I know I will be meeting her soon and I can't wait!"

Personally I am not religious, but I am certainly not an atheist. Giving advice on prayer may seem a bit questionable, but really, regardless if you believe that god makes things happen or have another name for it, the same principles apply.

CHAPTER 12

Finding the Observer and the Ego

We talked a lot about how things are, the human condition, and all the silly habits we have. We talked about how they make us feel and about the habitual nature of our feelings.

We discussed observation and how it can be a great tool to start getting our lives on the right track. Next, we'll look at pragmatic steps we can take to incorporate those ideas into our lives.

Since we are all very different, the path to consciousness we end up taking can vary. Instead of creating a step-by-step guide, this section contains various steps you can take that can help you, depending on where you are in the process.

It is enough to find one thing in this book that will stick, to help you make a significant positive change in your life. You can't fail any of the steps here, not pass, or miss a step and mess it all up. The steps illustrated here aim to invite you in to see if they speak to you or make sense. They aim to have you look at your life from a different angle and to describe the concepts that were previously discussed in a way that can help you incorporate them into your life.

The tips are organized like a toolbox. You can start by picking one and taking it for a spin, see if it speaks to you and if you can relate to it. You can't mess anything up!

With that said, take a deep breath, and jump right in.

FINDING OUR OBSERVER

Our observer is a conscious part of us. Our observer does not judge anything or see our reality or situation as good or bad, but it can reflect on what it observes. Observation is one of the most powerful tools we can use to bring about positive change to our lives, so learning how to find our observer and working with it is paramount. Our first exercise will be setting bait to the observer and then seeing it at work.

Our observer is always in touch with the universe and aware of the big picture. Our observer always knows an important truth about the past, future, and present: everything happened as it should have, everything will turn out exactly as it should, and right now, everything is always just right.

I know that things don't always seem right, and there certainly are things in the past that you believe went horribly wrong. But this is not so to our observer. Our observer sees the big picture beyond all that. It sees beyond drama, matter, and emotions.

Our observer has another distinct feature that allows it always to remain calm: it never judges anything. You can cut your hand on glass, and your observer will observe quietly. You can read horrible news in the paper or get into a fender-bender, and, regardless of the situation, the observer just observes quietly.

Each of us has our own observer, and if you have not yet had a chance to recognize your observer in you, then let's get to it.

While our observer is there all the time, like stars in the sky, it is much easier to recognize in the dark. Look back to a time when you were upset. Look through your memories of that time and see if you can track down that little silent voice that set on the side, looking, telling you that everything is all right.

Next, you're going to look forward to the next time you're upset (I know—can you not wait?). This time, even though you're upset, you are going to recognize that voice. It will not say anything particular. It will just be there as a part of your consciousness and observe. You can ask it, "Is everything really okay?" and it will just nod. It has no sense of humor whatsoever.

THE IMPORTANCE OF THE OBSERVER

Knowing that everything always turns out okay will make it so. Practicing that belief will slowly make it our reality. Since our observer already knows that, it can be a great ally in reminding us of that.

The observer, in some respects, is the opposite from the ego. While the ego tries to scream murder, blame, judge, and has a strong agenda, the observer does not.

Identifying with all the drama the ego throws at us causes the pain in our lives in one way or another. The cure starts with observation. Observation allows us to see the big picture, as it unfolds, without being trapped in it. Imagine falling into a pool and almost drowning. During that time we are in hysterics, we are trying to grasp onto something just to survive. At that point, nothing else matters, and it truly seems as if we could get really hurt.

Then, we find our observer, sitting there, watching the whole thing intently and not even getting nervous. At the beginning, we disregard it, but then we wonder if maybe it has a point. We enter its space and for a moment see things from its perspective. We observe not only the event, but also the emotions, and are surprised to see that this situation repeats itself every once in a while for various reasons.

This act of seeing events through our observer's eyes can heal the parts of us that crave the drama and push us into the pool time after time.

NOT APATHY

Knowing that everything is okay, as it is, does not mean we don't care dearly for people who suffer. In fact, it can allow us to be compassionate, caring, and helpful. We can do a better job helping people with pain when we aren't pulled into their life dramas.

The ego always has the selfish "what's in it for me" agenda. So even when we're helping someone, if the ego is involved, then we will be mostly helping ourselves.

THE REVOLT

As soon as we start to observe the ego, it will take notice. It knows things are changing, and to the ego, change in consciousness is like a ray of sunshine to a vampire. It feels the loss of control and revolts by increasing its efforts to control us with even more drama, more judgment, and more pain. It becomes more adamant about the separation between you and the people around you and may act in ways that can hurt your relationships.

Our ability to continue to observe depends on how deep we are in the ego's stronghold, how much we identify with it, and how dependent we are on the internal chemistry it wields.

When you manage to find your observer and peer at the world through its eyes, know that a storm is coming. Whenever there's real, positive change, there's also a storm. Know it, expect it, observe it, see through it, and love it.

FIND YOUR EGO

If you are the powers to be, and your subconscious is the powers to do, then your ego is the powers to be really annoying.

While our observer has one quiet form, the ego is loud, obnoxious, dramatic, and can sometimes be completely out of control. It can take on a million forms, has a spin ready for every possible situation, and is not embarrassed to use it.

Judgment is the tool the ego uses to wield its control—not only the judgment of people and events, but also judgment of the moment. Judgment of the moment is almost invisible and is not easy to identify. The ego's judgment is so well camouflaged that it seems as if the judgment is nothing but an integral part of the moment. Being stuck in traffic is annoying; coming in fourth or fifth in a race is discouraging; having things not go our way is upsetting. In reality, those three events are neither good nor bad, but the negative emotion gets attached to them so quickly that it appears as if they are one and the same. It takes some dissection to detach the judgment, and when we do, it has the ego's slime all over it.

I know, the word slime is judgmental, and it may be better to convey this message with as little judgment as possible. The truth is that the ego was created, in part, to protect us from being hurt, which is a notable goal. Unfortunately, even when we grow up and no longer need protection, the ego still does its best to keep us safe. Unfortunately, this happens at a great cost: at the other end of every rescue mission, there's always pain.

If we can separate the judgment from the event, we have found the ego. You will notice that the ego's signature is not only present when our pride is hurt or when we're acting selfish, but also in almost every aspect of our lives. For me—and most other people who live on this planet—the human condition dictates that we have a really annoying sidekick attached at the hip, yelling instructions, whispering criticism, pointing out problems, taking credit, and manipulating emotions. We can never fully get rid of it, and even mostly getting rid of it can take a lifetime. My goal, then, is to live with it happily ever after. If we can learn to live happily with our egos, we can live happily with any situation. Only the ego tells you not to live in peace. All you have to do is smile, nod, and say, "Thanks, but no thanks."

Recognizing judgmental and ego-infused elements in our minds are the first steps toward lowering the impact the ego has over our lives. I like to think that my ego is my Siamese twin, who is really talkative, means very well, and needs a lot of love. He's always full of advice that I have to pretend to consider before eventually disregarding it.

FIND OTHER PEOPLE

At times, it seems that the people around you are so different. People just around the corner can be into completely different things than you are. They can be practicing a religion that's totally foreign to you, be into sports or activities you know nothing about, belong to an opposite political party, and hold extremely different life views from you.

The differences between you and them that appear to have any importance or that are keeping you from being their best friend are all summed up by egos. In every person, there's a really sweet, compassionate, beautiful soul. It may be covered with a hard shell and embody a great amount of pain. It may appear as if they are holding a sign that says, "Stay the hell away from me." Underneath it all, they are not doing that. As you meet people and talk to them, look for the real person behind the positioning. See something in them that they can't even see in themselves. Completely listen to them without your own positioning. Understand where they are coming from and make an effort to observe your own judgment. Let them just be in your presence. You may be giving them a once-in-a-lifetime opportunity just to be (and surely your ego will take credit for that, but that's just what it does).

Inside every person, there's something really special; something you can connect with on a deep level regardless of the obstacles your and their egos are putting up along the way. See if you can find it—it's a fun game.

FIND THE JOY OF JUST BEING ALIVE

The good life does not lie hidden in the good things that happen to us. The good life is in how we feel. We become used to feeling good under certain situations, and it's great when those situations happen, but then other situations come along and knock the wind out of us.

While this may seem to be just the way things are, one crucial element is missing from this up-and-down life scenario. This element is the simple joy of living, the underlying current of good that is there all the time, which we can always tap into. We looked at it before and called it *being in the flow.*

Being in the flow transcends drama, life events, annoying morning commutes, being late to meetings, breakups, car dents, dead house plants, and broken dishes. It is not that you never feel bad. You do. It is just that through it all, there's a certain aspect of calm and understanding that all in the world is as it should be.

When you feel good in the flow and good things are happening, the sense of joy is much more relaxed and comfortable without the lurking anxiety that something bad will happen and ruin the fun.

A lot of this book focuses on this point, and most of what we looked at so far looks at the same thing from various perspectives—being in the flow, living the moment, being happy, the opposite of letting drama control our lives, listening to and identifying with judgment, letting the ego rule, etc. It's all the same—it all comes from the same source and has the same destination.

Eckhart Tolle said something brilliant relating to sin, or what Christ meant by it. He explained that to sin is to live an unconscious life ruled by our egos. This is a fundamental flaw in our human existence. Becoming aware of it and understanding that it's within our reach to fix can help us elevate our lives to amazing new levels.

Joy is not in things or events. Joy is not even the opposite of anything. Joy is just joy. It's locked inside you. Make it your life journey to figure out the combination. Joy is not likely to show up at your front door folded like a newspaper. Joy, and therefore a good life, is something you can pinpoint and say, "This is what I want." Money is important, as are a spouse, house, and car, but through it all, you have to decide that you want to be happy. You want to walk down the street and have people say, "What did this guy have for breakfast?"

Life, liberty, and the pursuit of happiness encapsulate our most cherished human rights, as brilliantly written in the U.S. Constitution. Life was given to us at conception, and as Westerners, we take liberty mostly for granted. We pursue happiness. On behalf of happiness, we have to clearly state, "This is something I want. I know it is inside of me now, and I am willing to figure out how to make it a part of my life." It's common to think that you can forget about happiness, get married, and make money and happiness is going to follow. Many take this road, and it ends with confusion and frustration. However, the opposite is quite true: when you find happiness inside you and have a joyful life, companionship will find you, and if money is something you want, it will find you as well.

CHAPTER 13

Strategies for Change

So, if we want to be happy, do we want to avoid being unhappy? Actually, it is quite the opposite. We want to look forward to being unhappy and accept it with open arms. We want to love being unhappy. This is true for a few reasons.

First, feeling bad is unavoidable; it is a part of our lives and a part of who we are. One important element of being aware is loving everything about our lives, including the bad parts. It is like taking medicine: we can resent it, deplore it, and suffer through it, or we can say "Cheers!" as we gulp it down and know we did something good for ourselves. There is no other sane alternative to loving everything in our lives, and that is especially true of the nasty parts.

After all, it's comfortable loving things that turn out our way. Feeling sad does not keep us out of the flow, but resentment does. Identifying with the message of negative emotions blocks us from being in the moment. For example, let's say that you're stressed because of money. This started with a thought and an influx of emotions that have similar energy and are connected. This was the uncontrolled part, an uninvited message from your subconscious via your ego. No matter what you do, these cautionary messages will always come in one form or another. Your reaction to those messages can take you out of the flow. Getting all upset because the reality is that you are having money problems and you cannot see the way out of them is now a choice. It may not have been a choice before, because a requirement for classifying something as a choice is that you are aware that it is a choice; well, you were just made aware of it.

So if the instinctual reaction is to become upset, what is the alternative? Remember that the source of those thoughts is your ego. What you can tell yourself in response is: "I know that even though money may feel tight right now, with a positive attitude and calming my anxiety, any issue will eventually resolve itself."

It could also be that the next step of stress and anxiety is so ingrained that it can't be stopped. That's okay! No matter how late in the process we observe ourselves, our thoughts, and our reactions, it is a start. It's like digging for a lost treasure. It may be covered with a foot of dirt, and it may be covered with five feet of gravel. The only choice is to start at the first point where we can observe the chain of events, emotions, and actions; own them 100 percent; and start melting them down. Being in the process, regardless of how long it takes, can already put us in the flow and make us feel good.

Bad feelings are like a thief; they come into our space and cause mayhem while we look the other way. A thief is difficult to catch when the he's not stealing. What we can do is go on a stakeout and hope to catch the thief in the act. We don't want the thief to steal, but the only way to catch him is in the act. The same goes for feeling bad. We don't want to feel bad, but knowing we certainly will at some point, we want to wait there and hope to be aware when it happens.

In this conversation, it is important to remember that our goal is not to abolish the institution of negative emotions. All we are looking to do is tweak our reactions to them when we do have them. The goal is to instill a sense that things in the world, and in your world, are always exactly as they should be. Knowing that our lives are good even when we feel bad is essential. Even when we're scared, confused, and feel like there's no way out, things are good. This method of feeling good about feeling bad and knowing things are good when they don't appear to be may seem a bit like forced self-delusion mixed with emotional masochism. It may be, but only through immersing ourselves in feeling bad and picking it apart from the inside, can we slowly melt it away. We can get to a point where we feel bad, but the emotions lack that horrible component of helplessness.

Negative emotions, such as anxiety, frustration, fear, and rage, are a repeating pattern for everyone. You want to be there when they happen. You want to be aware of them and get the most "bang for your buck," so to speak.

THE MIRROR TRAP

Many of the tricks in this book revolve around our egos. Our egos work by distracting us from what's important, knocking us unconscious, and altering our reactions to being angry, frustrated, annoyed, or any other reaction in its repertoire.

While the ego can run circles around us and have us do all sort of hideous things on its behalf, it is also rather predictable. One way to get a clue as to what we do when the ego takes over is to know how the ego is covering its tracks. One thing it does to make it difficult for us to admit or see that we react or act in certain unflattering ways is make us repulsed by the same behavior in other people.

You know, there are things that people do that we will like more and things they do we may like less. Then there are things people do that drive you nuts. Unfortunately, it is quite possible that those specific things drive us nuts because that is just the ego's reaction, and these are the exact things it makes you do.

In other words, if you want to know what annoying things you do, figure out what annoys you most about other people. It's not comfortable. After all, who wants to admit that they are aggravating or annoying, even sometimes? In the name of cutting to the chase and not beating around the bush, let's just say it now: we all act really annoying, regularly, and we have no idea that we do so. At least let's admit that. This is not a big deal, because if it were, your friends would have either told you by now or dumped you. And if it is bad, and they are trying to tell you or maybe already moved on, then you really better get out of the "bad stuff is happening to me" cloud and own the fortune you helped create.

Making our lives better almost always requires us to swallow a very large slice of humble pie. No way around it. You won't mind, though the ego is going to hurt a bit. Let it. Sit back and smile as you determine something for your ego just this once.

THE LOOP

There was one episode of *Star Trek: The Next Generation* that I often recall—episode 118. This one was completely different from any other episode. The entire story occurs during a short time span of less than a minute in which the USS Enterprise is destroyed. That minute is repeated. The last words are, "Abandon ship," and seconds later, everyone dies. Throughout the entire episode, that segment repeats, until the crew get hints that they are stuck in a loop and realize the minute keeps playing repeatedly.

During that span of one minute, the crew is trying to decipher a short, encoded message left by some unknown source. The crew later discovers they left the message in the time prior to their destruction. What saves them at the end is a message the android, Data, encodes into the loop that eventually gives him enough hints as to how to get out of the loop.

This episode is a lot like our lives. We are stuck in a loop where we are sometimes coherent, present, reasonable, and able to deduce, and other times, the ego knocks us unconscious, takes over, and wreaks havoc in our lives.

During that short time the ego takes over, it can create a horrible mess. We can be nasty to people that we love, spend our precious money, hurt our reputations, and ruin our careers.

Much like what Data did, we can leave encoded messages during our conscious time so we can possibly remember when we are under the ego's influence.

The depth of our unconsciousness during the part of the loop where we are unaware of our actions can vary greatly, depending on the severity of the event or situation that was the original cause of our condition. For example, dealing with an abusive parent can send us into deep unconsciousness where we can do horrible things and still believe we're a great parent to our own children. On the other hand, if a teacher in fourth grade made fun of you in front of the class and that brought about some odd shyness or related unconscious behavior, it may be easier to spot.

It may be that the unconscious stage is so severe that your ego is too protective, and it would take intervention such as hypnosis or other methods to deal with it.

Extreme cases aside, most people float somewhere in the light-moderate to heavy-moderate range. In those cases, it is quite possible to alter the way in which the reality loop recreates itself and reduce the effect that our egos have on our lives.

Earlier in the book, we discussed the positive effect that can be created when we observe the ego while it does its thing. This can be quite a shock, since the ego is used to having us asleep during that time. It can also be difficult since we are filled with convincing excuses as to why our actions—as ridiculous, selfish, or outrageous as they may be—are completely justified.

This particular trick involves planting a message during conscious time that we hope will be triggered during unconscious, ego-controlled time.

Let's look at an example where the subject has an issue with cleanliness. Being clean is fine, but that person becomes overly anxious about getting his shirt stained or something like that. Our subject is aware enough to know that his actions when he gets something on his clothes are over the top and can sometimes even hurt the person whose fault it is. However, when it happens, the ego takes over and our subject loses control and acts irrationally.

The subject, when aware, can say to himself, "I know I turn into a complete bastard when food touches my clothing. The next time that happens, I will just remember that I am being crazy. I can continue being crazy, but I will remember that the *aware me* is watching and would stop the behavior if he could."

Notice that we're not asking to stop the behavior, gain control, resist the urge to be mean, or anything drastic. This would have looked very strong and convincing but will be rather short-lived and quite impossible.

The real money is in tiny steps toward awareness. We want to melt our ego's control, one layer at a time. Once we feel more aware of our actions *while* they are taking place, we can move toward less passive messages, such as, "The next time I am hurting someone because of my irrational need for cleanliness, I will remember that no one ever died from a stain and that the cost of dry cleaning is much cheaper than losing or pissing off my friends."

Slowly and surely, messages we install during our aware time will penetrate and make themselves faintly visible during unconscious time. They will just sit there as a quiet truth. You will know that while it feels good to act like a complete jerk, the timer set to go off at the end of that part of your life is ticking.

THE MAGIC QUESTION

Through early observation, we learn that certain events and life situations cause an immediate anxious reaction. Logically speaking, anxiety is like a TV drama: we know it's not real and that it's a hypothetical scenario with a rather small chance of happening, but we still let it take over our emotions and believe the message that comes with it.

When anxiety strikes, there's a magical yes and no question we can ask right away. The action we take is in direct response to the answer we give, and it can help instantly relieve the stress.

The question is, is there anything I can or am willing to do right now to make this particular situation better? Call someone, make a plan, pay a bill, go to the pharmacy, etc. If the answer is yes, then do whatever it is, do it right away, and then forget about it.

If the answer is no, then forget just about it. Right at that moment, let it go. Holding it in your mind and letting it start a little tumor serves no positive purpose. It's only a habitual emotion that can, and most likely will, make you sick. It is also cyclical: spending time pondering stressful situations beyond our control and that we can't help at the moment brings on more such situations. While being immersed in them, we can't see that we can choose not to stew in that uncomfortable sensation.

This pragmatic question is amazing because it brings a sharp sense of logic into an emotional situation. After all, if there's nothing you can do, there's only one thing you must do: let go. Let go, let go, and then let go.

CHAPTER 14

Manifestation

Painting pictures in our minds is the one, pure creation tool we possess.

We have an amazing toolbox at our disposal. It is a toolbox with tools so powerful, they can spark the creation process of anything we could possibly want. It also has blocker agents that delay or inhibit creation.

HOW YOU CREATE WITH THOUGHTS

Is this really the heading of a section? It is more the title of a massive book series covering quantum physics, our physiology, and various other endless subjects. Whether our thoughts are confined to our brains and whether they happen in our brains to begin with or affect our surroundings and the universe is up for much debate.

We are at the dawn of understanding thought energy, so information is not as widespread as, say, dinosaur bones or proof the earth is round. There are also many scientists who would feel quite foolish when quantum mechanics is explained and our thought frequency measured and deciphered, so they prefer to stick their heads in the sand.

We are all very aware of how the big things in life work: you get shot, you lose blood—lose enough, and you die. Medical fact. We're not all that clear on the tiny things. We know that the laws of quantum physics turned the widely held Newtonian-Einsteinian laws on their heads. We discovered that instead of docile, little balls made of solid matter, underneath all the big things, little things are causing havoc. They appear, disappear, and can't be always pinpointed, and we don't even know what they are made of. Imagine—we don't know what the universe building blocks are! If you lived in a house, wouldn't you want to know if it is made of stone, wood, or, say, vibrant energy? Well, you can't. The answers are coming in, but even to know the little that has been discovered or proven so far you have to subscribe to the newest science publications, and read a lot of them. What the universe is made of, and all matter in it, including us, is still being discovered. There are theories, such as string theory, that give plausible ideas, but there is no Eureka moment yet.

What is as clear as a bell is that the universe is not made of solid atoms. It is rather made of mostly of nonmatter, such as energy, empty space, or what-have-you. By "mostly," I don't mean like maybe two-thirds or 95 percent. By "mostly," I mean that from what we know, the universe matter accounts for 0.0000000000001 of its volume. Imagine, what we thought was made of "stuff" is simply not. It's made of mostly nothing. This is also not referring to the vast volume of empty space; this is referring to what we consider solid matter, such as cars, dirt, stone, human flesh, etc.

What scientists also know very well is that human thoughts and intentions affect our surroundings. There is no argument about it; it's more a matter of how much we affect it. We know we can't will a pile of bricks to become a wall by simply looking at them, but we know with certainty that we change the behavior of subatomic particles by simply observing them, whether we want to or not. Now doesn't it somehow make sense that if we can manipulate and affect the tiniest building blocks of the universe with our thoughts, we can affect the bigger things made out of those blocks? Makes enough sense to me.

Regardless of your scientific understanding, once you learn, even just a little bit, about how to use your mind to create your life, there will be no doubt left in your mind.

Wait a minute...can we will those bricks into a wall?

As I reread what I wrote earlier about not being able to turn bricks into a wall with our thoughts, I've realized that it's a false statement. In fact, I will take it a step further by saying: there is no other way to build a brick wall.

Too radical for you? Okay, then let me give you this challenge: show me a wall made of construction bricks, anywhere or anytime in the history of the world, that was not first imagined by a human. No such thing exists. And why? Because creation first happens in one's imagination. The physical process that follows is the manifestation of that initial creation process.

Now show me something you personally created that you did not first imagine in some way. Right. I thought so.

This brick wall, of course, stands for anything and everything we want to create in our lives. It always starts with imagining it, intending to have it happen without any doubt, and then allowing the physical creation process to take place.

REALISTIC EXPECTATIONS

We discussed the process of creation and talked about how everything in the universe is made of energy. We also talked about things we consider unattainable, such as lots of money right away when we don't have it, someone really cute to be with when we are lonely, etc. According to the theory, if everything is energy and we can summon energy using the power of our thoughts and intentions, making a million dollars should be theoretically as easy as finding a penny on the floor.

Theoretically, it is, but you are a person with a mind, a past, and a certain reality, not a hypothetical being. While all material is made of energy that you can interact with, your bandwidth of attracting various things is only constrained by your beliefs. The easiest things to believe you can achieve are, of course, things you have already achieved. For example, if you wanted a sandwich, you would just go to the store, get bread, tomato, lettuce, and mustard, and make yourself a sandwich. You would not even consider the magic that has just happened! You're biting into processed wheat that grew somewhere in Montana, the water in your tomatoes is rain that fell in Mexico a few weeks ago, and the mustard was little yellow flowers in a Nepal field at around the same time. You then combined it all in a creative process into a food that fit your taste perfectly.

While this is a great achievement, it was easy to do for one reason: you had no doubt you could do it. If you had no doubt, right now, that you could make a million dollars by next month, then you could do that too, just as easily.

A new scale is starting to emerge: instead of the range of what is possible, we can look at a range of what *we believe* is possible. This scale can help us determine what should make a good intention project. Pick something just outside of your comfort zone.

For instance, if I told you to manifest ten dollars, you could do it easily, because much like making a sandwich, you have little to no resistance to the idea that you can do it. On the other hand, if I said that you should manifest a million dollars, not a single bone in your body will believe that can happen. Therefore, the resistance to that idea is too great to overcome using simply the power of your intention. So manifesting, say, a hundred dollars may be a good project.

Other projects can involve getting tickets for a sports game, having a pleasant and unexpected social interaction, or anything else not in your current plans. Make it better than something that happens in your life, but not something that appears totally impossible.

A realistic intention is just that—an intention within the realm of what appears possible.

The point is to start smaller and as you gain confidence in your ability to manifest situations or things in your life, look further.

KNOWING WHEN A GOAL MAKES SENSE

We are all born with an aptitude, some unique pull in a specific direction that is a part of who we truly are. We discussed that earlier, in the *Genius* section. It may be working with animals, it may be teaching, wielding steel, managing finance, painting, making cloths, or miming. It can be almost anything.

This direction is something we were born with, and we can potentially do really well in it. Finding out what it is, and immersing ourselves in it, is a condition for a happy life.

When our goals are in line with our aptitudes, nothing can stand in our way of getting it, and our responsibility is to set our intentions on getting it, regardless of what anyone else says or thinks.

If you love animals but have no ability to cook, you may be a complete failure flipping burgers for minimum wage, but you'll be able to run your own veterinary clinic successfully. You know what you're destined to be doing because it makes you feel like no other thing does and has since childhood. Think back to what subjects fascinated you as a child and find a connection to what you love to do today.

A goal in line with your true potential cannot be impossible to achieve, and if you go after it, you'll have help from unexpected sources. There's an entire support chain ready to propel you forward when you decide to go into that specific field. Find out what it is and jump in.

BASIC INTENTION IS ALWAYS GOOD AND NOW

Intention is fun and easy: sit and imagine, in the most positive terms, what you want and how great it feels to have. Notice I didn't say *will have*. I said *have*.

Our subconscious takes instructions in the form of a description linked to positive feelings in the present. Remember what Janis Joplin said, "Tomorrow never happens, man, it's all the same f***ing day." She knew something fundamental there, and the subconscious works the same way. If we imagine having things in future tense and imagine how we will *feel in the future* when we finally have it, the subconscious is not going to respond. However, an intention described as *happening now*, and if we feel great about it now, gets processed right away as the active plan on the subconscious to-do list.

The basic intention-based creation process looks like this: you, sitting down in a quiet place, closing your eyes if you're able, imagining as if you already have that thing you want, and feeling amazing about it.

Surprise! We're going to practice this right now.

Think of something you really want. It can be anything, but for this exercise, I want you to go a step beyond your comfort zone. If it's a car, make it a Porsche, if it's a girlfriend, make it Keira Knightley; and if a career, go for editor of O Magazine. I realize that these are probably not in your range of feasibility, but I have a point I want to make, so bear with me.

Sit back and, in the most positive and present way, imagine having or being that thing. Focus on the joyful feeling having that thing gives you. That positive feeling is the fuel that will shoot your intention further.

Observe the fundamental difference between resenting not having something and the joy of having it. Resentment is one of the top blockers, and the joy of having now, well, it is the most powerful creation tool we can have.

So is that it? If creating is so easy, why do most people not have everything they want? Because while it is that easy, the main factors blocking intention from materializing are doubts storming our thoughts.

Doubts, anxiety, microdetails, social considerations, monetary realities, and general feelings of not being deserving enough will shift our thoughts from what the ego may consider unnecessary and distracting goals. Our own thinking will separate us from our desires.

INTENTION PURIFICATION

Imagine describing your plan to a team of people whose job it is to make it happen. They are highly regarded professionals and can make whatever plans you envision happen.

The only information you want to give them is the description of your plan and some words to inspire them.

Leave out any negativity. Don't share any skepticism that they can do it. Avoid sharing your doubts and concerns—remember, they can do anything. You also don't want to micromanage. Don't get into *how* things should be done because they know that part much better than you do. Follow the process while trusting that the work will be done to your satisfaction.

The same is true when describing an intention to the subconscious. When we use visualization, we are actually triggering the process of creation by describing our goal to the subconscious. The subconscious, being about a million times faster and more capable than the conscious mind, can perform anything we ask. The important thing to understand is that the subconscious can't differentiate between a vision and a doubt. For the subconscious, it all sounds like instruction.

To better understand this, let's pretend that you want a new sports car and decide to manifest it using visualization. You sit and imagine yourself driving the new car. Then, as soon as your ego catches wind of that, it starts to slip in its two cents by saying, "This is far beyond my reach," "I am not able to make the payments because I'm already in debt," "People will judge me for driving a car," "No one will give me a loan for that," etc. Since these all sound like realistic thoughts, you identify with them, and soon enough, your fun visualization turns into an anxiety session where not having the car starts to seem much better than all the trouble it will bring.

Now, that just might be in your benefit! We were not meant to have every single thing we want, and giving up on some ideas is a good thing.

Regardless, our egos will interrupt all our intentions, not just the ones we weren't meant to have! The ego's goal is to keep things as they are, and if a goal breaks that boundary—and most worthy goals do—we have to develop a method of purifying our intentions from the "realistic," unhelpful take of your ego.

ONLY THOUGHTS

This would be a great time to remember that our egos can sometimes be our opinionated conjoined twin. Viewing the ego that way and assigning to it all the negative commentary disguised as realism will allow us to cast those thoughts aside and focus on visualization and intention.

Let's look at an example again. So you decide that a new sports car *is* really what you desire. You sit down and give visualization another shot. You happen to be in your old car when you get the idea to visualize, so you imagine that you are actually driving your new sports car. You can smell it, touch the steel gearshift, and hear the engine respond to the accelerator. Then a discouraging, "realistic" thought passes through: "The payments are going to be half your income."

Up until now, your reaction would be to understand that this can't really happen. Your new attitude, however, is this: "This was just a thought. Right now, I don't have to bother with these details or anxieties. All I need is to enjoy visualizing."

Observing our thoughts instead of believing them is a skill that takes some getting used to. We're taught from a very young age to believe our thoughts and not question them. There is also a strong emphasis in our society on *being realistic* and not being *a dreamer.* The people who tell us to be realistic are trying to push their own reality on us, possibly to keep us back. They may not mean anything bad by it, or they may be trying to protect us, but they are definitely not helping us move forward.

Remember this important fact: our reality is the reality we create. Go and create a really fun one!

FUELING INTENTION

The intention itself is the direction we want to go, the specific thing or situation we want to manifest. While a direction is good, we need to put some serious energy behind the intention.

Don't worry, that energy is not the old "go and get them, Tiger!" advice you'd surely get elsewhere. The energy comes in the form of powerful joyful, positive emotions.

Emotions send waves of energy that take on whatever flavor our thoughts have and propel them across the room and across the universe. Those waves will find energy of similar makeup and stick to it. This is the law of attraction working, and it works for negative and positive emotions.

In this case, we want to intentionally put positive emotions to work for us. We want the energy in emotions such as awe and gratitude to shoot out, spread, and deliver our message. We want the subconscious to be saturated with the signature of the thoughts and emotions we emit when making our intentions known.

GRATITUDE

One of the most powerful things we can do to advance the manifestation of intention is be grateful. There are powerful vibes involved in feeling grateful, and they can instantly transform our moods and the moods of people around us as well as bring back a similar sentiment.

Try it right now to see the effect it can have. Find something small you can be grateful about, and, well, be grateful. This is not a light suggestion; this is something we *are* going to do right now.

Think about that one thing you are happy about having, even if it's something everyone has, such as being able to breathe, play softball, kiss your kids, feel the wind—anything.

Now take that feeling of gratitude, hold it in your mind, and press the gas pedal. Can you feel it? Now, as this amazing feeling of gratitude washes over you, focus on being grateful for that feeling. Do you now see what I mean? Gratitude is one thing you can never go wrong with.

Whenever we think about how we can move life forward, sensing immense gratitude is always a good bet.

AWE AND AMAZEMENT

How many things do we have as people on this beautiful earth that we take for granted? We walk around complaining like spoiled brats about how not everything is up to our standards and how things are not always going our way.

The focus of our intentions can be a great place to be amazed again. That thing you always wanted, imagine having it right now, and being amazed and awestruck about getting it so effortlessly. Forget about what you used to call *reality*, just focus on the desire for the subject of your intention. Be in awe at how fun it is to have that thing. This energy is fueling the creation process, making subatomic particles form into matter as you are sitting there, imagining.

JOY

The joy we feel when manifesting our intention should be so pleasurable that it can be the reward itself! Not that we want to have the feeling and not the thing, but the intensely good feeling should be a reason all by itself to practice visualization. Knowing that we are actually manifesting that same thing we're imagining is an extra bonus. It should be like the stereotypical entrepreneur lying in a hammock in Hawaii while his business runs itself and makes him money.

Remember, joy is its own reward. If we can feel joyful simply by imagining what we want, we are already there.

CHAPTER 15

What Can I Do Right Now?

Now that we have all these amazing visualization tools available to us, let's use them.

Many times during the week, I find myself asking what I can do right now to advance my goal. The answer is always the same, and I can't think of a better one: visualize.

When you are not in the middle of something and wish to advance your cause, do the only thing you can do that the subconscious can't do: imagine. The subconscious is like a powerful car, boat, and airplane in one; it can take us anywhere we can imagine, but it cannot set the direction. You, however, can do the imagining. It doesn't take hours a day, and there's no rule or regimen to follow other than what we decide.

We have to restate our goals and reiterate them to the subconscious because the "thought gravity" always pulls the subconscious toward existing core beliefs and complementary habits, such as stress, anxiety, and little everyday fears.

In space, we can push an object once, and it will continue indefinitely. Much like the friction that will eventually stop any object you push here on earth, the subconscious will start to follow other messages we unintentionally send it.

Remind the subconscious what you're looking to achieve as often as you can. At first, you will not always remember to, and that's okay. Make an effort to remember to visualize once or twice a week. Remember that the ego has an interest in keeping the status quo, and it will always try to get us to stop by distracting us and pulling our attention to other things.

The key is not to expect consistently being able to practice it because you decided to give this a shot. It is possible, but any time you practice visualization, you are making a difference.

If you are set on a schedule and get distracted, the lack of progress may be discouraging. Remember that real progress is very slow. Enjoy the times you do get to visualize rather than think you're not doing enough.

MANTRAS

Having a few simple mantras helps me in this whole business of awareness and enlightenment. They are something I can always fall back on when my thinking feels clouded.

Mantras are not secret mantras given by a guru in exchange for thousands of dollars or bought on a CD via the Web. They are our own little phrases that we make up or pick up along the way. The mantras can remind us to stay on course and not be swayed by anxiety, frustration, and other habitual blockers.

Mantras are not supposed to go against anything or help us resist feeling bad. We can feel perfectly horrible while having a simple mantra, such as *everything is always good*, sit in the corner and smile at us. We do not want the good of the mantra to push away the bad we feel; it is only a reminder to put what we feel in perspective.

Here are some of my personal favorite mantras. They are really simple. They are mantras not because they are divinely worded or were found under a rock in the Himalayas, but because I use them.

When I'm stressed or anxious about something, I use this one: *everything always turns out well.* It helps me realign myself and keeps my emotions in perspective. It reminds me that the other me, the one that's relaxed and content and not swept by emotions as I am at that point, is watching over me and wishing me well. It reminds me that my feelings are not reality and will be passing soon. It also doesn't urge me to feel better. Sometimes you need to feel like crap, and sometimes it feels nice to feel like crap. Don't feel the need to rush it. It's a bit like how it's nice to hold your breath and dive underwater when you know there's lots of air just above you, and you will be able to breathe it as soon as there's no more oxygen in your lungs.

A mantra I often use is not attached to any particular situation. This mantra is simply: *allow.* I usually close my eyes and just repeat it again and again, as I imagine my inner blocks melting. This mantra helps me get back in the flow. It reminds me that goodness is not something hidden I have to search for, or even something I have to reach for, but rather something that is coming to me all the time.

A nice and simple mantra for when I am overloaded with obsessive, pointless thoughts is: *let go.* Stupid thoughts can be like that fly ringing in your ear. You wave them off, and a second later, they are there again, interrupting your quiet.

Occasionally, for example, I get the idea that something small my wife is thinking is the reason I am feeling bad at the time.

Of course, this is all in my head, not hers, so she has nothing to do with it. Once I had an argument with her in my mind, and finally I told her in response to her response (again, all in my mind), "This is just ridiculous!" At this point, I caught myself and thought, "Yup, sure is. I made up an entire fight with my wife in my own head. Ridiculous."

At these times, when you suddenly realize that your mind is taking you for a really pointless ride, repeating the mantra *just let go* again and again is really helpful.

I use another mantra when I have some down time. Any time I need to recharge, my mind just sort of shuts down. I have no creative ability and no ability to get up and do anything. I just move from the bedroom to the TV room to the sofa checking e-mail (knowing I have none), and back again. My ego, of course, is going nuts, saying, "What do you mean, do nothing? You should be working to move things forward!" My mantra for that is: *as soon as I should, I would.* This reminds me that what I have created and made happen so far was not due to trying or making an effort, but rather due to allowing myself to flow with things, to be in the *present.* It reminds me that what I should be doing at any point is exactly what I *happen to be doing.*

If a thought about doing something specific comes to me, I quickly deploy my magic question: *Is this is something I can or am willing to do right now?* If the answer is no, I let it go. If the ego keeps harassing me with "should," I repeat my mantra: *as soon as I should, I would.* That reminds me that doing nothing is actually recharging and is an important component of creation.

RESIST NOTHING

We talked about resisting as one of the important aspects of noncreation, stagnation, and pain. We should talk about it again.

Resistance is one of the top flow-blockers. Being in a mental state of resistance doesn't just mean that there's something in the present situation that we are discontent with; it means that we are actively in contention with our situation. We can, for example, be sad and still be in the flow and not resist being sad. Resentment is the disagreeable response to a situation. Resistance means you prefer to be somewhere else, doing something else.

Even when we are in a less than ideal situation, we cannot be anywhere else doing anything else. If you can, and you know how, then by all means take action right away. Many times, however, we find ourselves in a situation we prefer not to be in, but since we either see no recourse or choose not to take action, we resent that situation. This resentment and frustration with *what is*, is the cause for our resistance, and therefore the cause for not being in the flow.

If we want to be in the flow and move in the direction of peace of mind, joy, and being able to allow goodness to come, we must observe resistance and actively love everything.

Love whatever situation you are in, even if it stinks. This takes some practice. Loving everything doesn't mean jumping up and down with joy every time we stub our toe or running to thank our boss after we are fired. It means finding the part that knows that everything we experience is a part of life, and that living life is amazing. A part of you already knows that and is ready to share it with you.

It may appear as if loving uncomfortable things will bring more of them and resisting them will keep them away. The opposite is true. The only sane thing to do is to love and let go. Let go.

PREPARE FOR INTERNAL RESISTANCE

We discussed the various reasons the subconscious and ego are interested in keeping things the way they are. For one, we may decide to take our lives in a positive direction, but the subconscious will still be working from negative habits created in the recent past.

The ego, on the other hand, is freaked out when we start to become more aware because we start to step on its toes and encroach on its territory.

Once we decide to move in a positive direction, we have to be willing, happy, and ready to be emotionally abused from the inside. Habitual thinking and other forces mentioned may throw everything at us so we return to the comfortable unconsciousness we were immersed in.

Think back to the movie The Matrix and what Neo had to go through once he realized he was dreaming and decided to wake up. It was really ugly, and the new reality was dark and uncomfortable, but it was still far better than anything the matrix could offer. Being aware is not always comfortable, and sometimes downright uncomfortable, but it is always worth it. Being fully present is another level of being, and we want to be a part of it regardless of the obstacles.

RELAPSE WITH JOY

When behavioral change happens, a set of relapses will follow. No matter what we do or how firmly we hold on, old habits and thought patterns will catch up with us. Don't fight, and if you find yourself fighting, let go. Don't be frustrated because it is a part of the process, and when you do find yourself getting frustrated, remember that the only sane thing to do is to love everything. Love that you are changing, then love that you are relapsing, then love that those relapses frustrate you, and mostly, love it that you can observe it all and smile about it. Resistance is futile. New habits will sink in and relapses will become more subtle and rare. Old thought patterns and reactions will always be there holding your hand and walking with you; they will just not be as annoying.

LET GO

Finally, the one step without which nothing else is possible: letting go. We discussed it throughout the book, but being one of the cornerstones of your new life, it is important to look at again.

We are working on cleansing ourselves from episodes of anxiety, doubt, and fear. We are setting goals in line with our inner brilliance, and we have set distinct intentions.

Who is going to make all this happen? Who is going to do the work required to put you in the state of mind and life situation you want to be in?

While our hands, legs, and mouths will be doing most of the ground work, controlling any of it is not our job. In fact, none of it will happen if you attempt to micromanage or control the process.

Good things happen only when we let them. Good things happen when we let go of the need to control.

Once we are on the path of cleansing ourselves, we have to seriously observe our instinctive need to control and "make things happen." We have to let go, or our actions will be the reasons life keeps dragging behind instead of shooting forward.

The innate need we have to control—the obsessive thoughts and feelings that tell us to try and make an effort rather than trust—is a tough one to get over. As soon as we sit down under a tree without a sense of purpose, just observing the beauty, our egos start to yell at us to get our butts moving and "do something."

Making things happen in life is like tending to a potted plant. We make sure we have a plant that can survive, put it in some good dirt in a sunny spot, water it every few days, and maybe move it around a couple of times a year. The rest is trusting that the plant will grow. Forcing more actions on the plant can only kill it.

Trust, let go, trust, let go, and then let go some more.

CHAPTER 16

More Given Things to Question

Being aware of and following social conventions allows us to live in society with minimal friction. Some conventions are stricter than others are, and some societies have different ways of doing things. For example, in my New England neighborhood, you will not catch anyone walking around naked, but you do see people wearing minimalistic clothes here and there. It varies, but it is regulated by the society's unwritten code. I know there are laws against walking around naked, but I doubt that anyone would, even if it were legal. In Scandinavia, on the other hand, people see nothing wrong with baring it all, and on the other side of the world, not being completely covered can cost a woman her life. These conventions are not a bad thing. For the most part, I can choose to live almost anywhere, and Providence fits perfectly. But we have to watch for a different kind of societal convention: conventions that are a big part of how we think and that cover large geographical areas.

For example, take the ideas of competition, winning, blame, revenge, and struggle. Are these just integral parts of being human? Sure seems like it. Can you live without them? And if you could, would you want to?

The following sections question such conventions, evaluate them, and determine whether we could possibly live without them.

SHOULD

When the word *should* is used in the context of planning or teaching, it is perfectly acceptable. In everyday life, however, when used with a first or second person noun, the word *should* is saturated with regretful emotions and smells of missed opportunities. *I should have been there, I should have done that, you should really have,* etc.

Really, you shouldn't have simply because you couldn't have. There is no other way to do things other than the way they happened. Putting any regretful emotions behind a decision you made may play a role in what happens in the future but not in the direction you may expect.

The decisions you made at any given point were a reflection of who you were at that time. If you want to make different decisions, work on being a different person. Until then, no matter how much you beat yourself up for this bad decision, you will keep on making those same decisions.

Another way we use *should* is when we start a sentence with, "I really should…" Are we being genuine or just sparking up some drama? Give it up—if you should have done something else, you would have. Otherwise, buck up, slap on a smile, and own your actions so you will be less likely to repeat them.

ꕤ

PROBLEMS

Problems are fun. From the inside, they look so dark, special, and dramatic. But they are all sort of the same from the outside. This is not intended to show you that I find your problems boring and overdramatic; it is intended to have you possibly think that.

As everything else in our worldly lives, problems are our doing. We look at what is an objective event, declare it to be a problem, declare ourselves the victims, and go on a round of self-pity. I have a problem here; I have a problem there. No, you don't. We have brought these situations in our lives in some way. These situations may need immediate handling, or not. Either way, feeling down because of these things called problems is just playing into the master plan: being upset and bringing on more of the same.

It's tough to blame anyone since those situations, in some way, originated from us. It's also silly to blame ourselves because we did not knowingly do anything wrong. So we're going to put away the blaming finger altogether and think about what to do.

There are two aspects here: (1) the matter of the issue that needs resolution, and (2) ending the cycle that made this issue come up in the first place.

Most important for now, though, is how we feel. Changing our state from victim to confidently in charge is important. By doing that, you will be sending your subconscious a clear message: getting upset by everyday events is the old me. The new me knows that everything is good and that everything always turns out just fine, even if sometimes I need to take actions that don't feel great, and even if I sometimes don't feel great.

I realize that there are big issues, such as having a serious disease. These issues, though, are not much different. Any disease your body has is most likely the result of what you feed your body or what you feed your mind. In those circumstances, a solid dose of positivity is just what the doctor ordered. Only by changing the outlook from negative to positive will you be able to do right by all the other decisions you need to make.

STRUGGLE

Struggle is another habitual human state. We pick it up from our parents, extended family, or small town. We learn that nothing in life comes easy, and guess what? When that is what we believe, that is what our lives will look like.

When we buy into the struggle paradigm, we will no doubt have a life full of it. I've never heard anyone say, "Gee, life is full of struggle, but I somehow escaped it, and my life is easy." When we believe that struggle is an unavoidable part of life, our reality will reflect it.

So please tell me if struggle is a fact of human existence, why are there people who truly do not experience struggles? Are they not human?

The answer is simple: when our lives are a struggle, at some point, we have bought into the fallacy. I am telling you right here and now that life is not a struggle. Life is good and can be fun and joyful, and not only after we're done dealing with the crap. It can be joyful most of the time. If you are stuck in a struggle, it might be quite difficult to escape, but taking the first step is always within reach. In fact, you are taking it right now!

ꕥ✦ꕥ

FAULT

Perhaps blame is one of the best defense mechanisms we possess and masterfully put to use. As humans, we hate the idea that we are responsible for anything negative so much that the ego, at first sight of trouble, finds the most possible party to blame. This can be a person, an event, a place, an object, a group of people, etc. No matter what the situation is, the greatest threat to our egos may be that it will be perceived as our fault.

I remember playing soccer as a kid. I sucked. I stuck to being the goalie; somehow having to deal with only two dimensions seemed more manageable. I remember one game where right as we had to go back to class, I scored a self-goal. Instantly my mind found three players whose fault it was that I scored that goal. I remember my good friend telling me, “You always find someone else to blame.” Wow, that was a solid reality check. I was upset at first, but I remember from that point starting to pay attention to my blaming thoughts.

The opposite is also possible and is just as unhelpful: we may compulsively blame ourselves right away. This blame, although closer to what actually happened, is still not helpful and is usually full of self-pity.

Somewhere inside, we know that we are responsible for anything we are involved with. Since we don’t live in a vacuum, most unpleasant things have another party involved. If we are hurt, our instincts are to blame either ourselves or someone else. . Whether it’s the closest person or as far out as God.

Americans grow up knowing that justice means suing something or someone as soon as anything goes wrong. If there is a person or a company at the other end of the fiasco, it is their fault. It is time to find a good lawyer and sue them. Victimhood in this country can make you rich and famous. We are taught from an early age to avoid responsibility at any cost and to pull the victim card.

In corporations, the institution of blame has reached such a level of importance that self-preservation by never admitting fault is much more important than the well-being of the company itself. As long as my butt is covered, I am good. Instead, companies should commend people who take chances and accept responsibility when things don't turn out. In an atmosphere of fear, creativity and growth are stifled. This has to start from the top, but rarely does.

Evaluating the concept of blame, though, is most important in our personal lives. Seeing things that happen as someone's fault and being quick with a pointed finger helps us miss the big picture. We have to understand that our lives are in our hands. We are the only ones who can make a difference in our own lives. We are the only ones that can steer it in a different direction.

On the other hand, we are not at all responsible for other people, unless they are our direct responsibility, such as our kids or students or if we are their guides, managers, etc. Telling another adult how they should have behaved and pushing our package of responsibility to their side of the court can only have a negative effect on everyone involved.

We can help them move on and be an amazing example for how good things in this world are created. Either forgive or apologize. Sincerely and wholly, voicing your responsibility in whatever happened, and if they wronged you in any way, do whatever it is you need to do to forgive them and move on. Forgiveness has the power to change someone forever. Someone who otherwise would expect you to jump all over them and blame them for everything that is wrong, someone in a full defensive position, can really use a good dose of forgiveness. Forgiveness and understanding can be healing, and wherever the other person is in their life right now, it can help him or her move forward.

On the other hand, if you have any part in the event, express your apologies as sincerely as possible after the storm is over. There seems to be a universal resistance and fear of apologizing or expressing concern. Saying, "I am sorry" will most likely not make the other person jump up and say, "Ah-ha! It was your fault! Hell, am I ever going to get you now, and I have the whole thing on tape!" For the most part, people want to be heard and understood. They want to know that you saw that they are hurting and that we empathize with them. However, if they do give you the finger and sue you, there's nothing you can do about it. This is their decision and would have happened anyway. We do not have to behave as if we expect the worst of humankind just in case the person we are dealing with is the worst. Be the bigger person and make everything a little better for everyone. Consequently, you will make things a little better for yourself.

FAIRNESS AND ENTITLEMENT

Oh, justice for all! What is it based on, if not on the most objective value of all: fairness? One problem with this, though. We can be on opposite sides of the exact situation and what seems fair to me seems unfair to you, and the other way around. And the worst thing is, the other person is just as right as you are.

Being obsessed with fairness hardly ever seems to come from people who believe that they came up on top. Most people who cry that life is unfair believe that they are entitled to more than their current share.

Here's a news flash for you, and unless things are hunky-dory for you, you really need to listen: life is always perfectly fair. I know, this seems to be the statement of a white, middle-class guy who doesn't lack anything. From a certain perspective, it may appear to be true, and it may be comfortable to think. However, let us look at it from a proactive angle rather than from a victim angle.

The first fact we have to make clear is that being a victim may feel good momentarily and as if we are right and seeking justice, but it has an opposite side. Being a victim is more likely to get us more of the same stuff that made us into a victim in the first place. There are no victims. There are only people who see themselves as victims. I know, I am really stepping in it now, and I prefer not to avoid that issue. Out of all the groups in this country, the *victim* victim group is the most protected. Pointing out anything that is other than, "Oooh, look at the poor victim" is just plain mean. We can be a victim of a crime, a policy, a war, or any other thing that leaves behind victims, but we don't have to fall into a victim state. Being in a victim state is a chronic way of being, much like refusing to use deodorant.

These statements are not meant to be offensive to people who are suffering, but rather to point out the first necessary step to a better life: own it. Own everything about your life. Own the good, the bad, and the ugly. Say aloud that as uncomfortable as it may be, in some unknown and unseen way, something in you brought your life to what it is.

Then, stop blaming anyone else. Stop crying that life is unfair. Stop whining about what you deserve. This will bring you a whole bunch more of the stuff you're complaining about.

A simple mathematical equation can help us understand why life appears to be so unfair.

What we deserve = who we think we are + what we don't know about ourselves

In short, we always get from life exactly what we deserve. Own it. If our tendency is to complain, blame, or bathe in our spectacular victimhood, then know that life will give us plenty to complain about.

If you want your life to change for the better and you want to have fewer things you consider unfair, forget about fairness altogether. Forget about justice, forget about entitlement, forget about what you think you deserve, because as long as you don't have it, you don't deserve it.

Start loving your life right now. Find something to like about it, like the fact that everything about it is about to change. Love it, be grateful, and find someone to hug and say thank you. Live now. Be.

ജ•ഗ

COMPLAINING

Complaining is a great American pastime. It is like the lollipop we get as consolation prize after losing. We sit there, pouting; the winner may have the medal, but we are the ones with the sugary stick.

Complaining is the universal entitlement. It is free and feels so good. We often hear the phrase "I deserve to complain." If you think you deserve to complain when things don't go your way, you are right. When you stub your toe on a rock, you also deserve to kick that rock back, really hard. The question rising from both scenarios is why would you ever want to? Let's start with why we would want to observe our own complaining.

Complaining is the stuff that more bad stuff is made of. Complaining is telling our story to the universe under the title of "Things I want more of." Whenever we're complaining, we're sending a vibe. This vibe carries the contents of our complaining and the energy put behind it. The vibe is mainly comprised of the sentiment that life keeps dishing us one bad thing after the other.

Maybe the biggest excuse to complain is that it's the only little pleasure we can take when something bad happens in our lives. We can get a little attention and feel good for a minute despite the unpleasant situation we're complaining about. True, there's nothing wrong with sharing a bad experience once in a while in exchange for some comfort and attention. It's when complaining becomes an automatic conversation you have with people that you know it's detrimental.

Here's an exercise: suggest to yourself that you do away with complaining and then observe your own reaction to that idea. If it's almost as if I suggested you give up TV or your morning coffee, you most definitely want to give complaining a serious look. View it and treat it as a habitual thought pattern that is a big part of what you don't like in your life.

Habitual complaining is not a harmless activity. Picture this: you are sitting in the proverbial restaurant of the universe. The waitress shows up and asks you for your order. Instead of ordering, you tell her about everything that's wrong with your life, to which she answers, "Thank you for your order, sir. It will be up soon."

৯•৫

EXCUSES

Excuses are great. If we can come up with a somewhat legitimate line that explains why a certain situation is acceptable, then it is acceptable. We make up amazing excuses for anything and everything. We have a constant need to justify our every step—things that came out wrong, why we did or didn't do something, and why it was okay to hurt someone, not work out, eat that candy bar, etc. Sometime the excuse is made up before the action ever took place.

Then there are inexcusable things. What in the world does that mean? Does it mean the person doing them could not possibly come up with an explanation as to why they did? We do very few things in life that we can truly explain.

We don't make excuses for everything, though. There are things that happen in our lives in which we have a hand that we don't feel any need to explain. We do feel the need to explain and make excuses for elements in our lives that are a part of a negative pattern. If you take all the things you make excuses for and chart them over a couple of months, I guarantee that you will come up with something that looks a lot like the things that are wrong in your life. It may be food, career, relationships, parenting, or other habits. We make excuses for things we do that add to the negative cycle of our lives.

Excuses can be difficult to identify. As soon as our minds come up with the excuse, and the self-justification drug takes hold, we believe completely that there's full justification to our actions. When the mind is making up excuses, it is trying to hide something quite significant.

How do you know excuses are a bad sign? Simple: the actions you take that are just right and put you in the flow never seem to need justification! Do you ever say, "Hmm…I really deserve to go out for a run," or "I earned that salad, and I don't care what anyone says. I was really good and haven't had a vegetable for a whole week"? When things are right, we do them, enjoy them, live them, and fully experience them. When things are not right, we need to justify them with stories.

Instead of trying to identify which justifications are legitimate and which are excuses, why don't we just question the whole idea of self-justification? Whenever I catch myself telling myself stories about why it is actually right of me to do this and that, I immediately call my own bluff. Now, I realize that I don't always catch myself, and when I do, sometimes all I can do is sit back and watch it as it happens. Nonetheless, observing this flavor of mind activity, and being present while it takes place, enhances our abilities to catch it in the act. When we are aware that our minds are making excuses, we are actually reducing the excuse effectiveness and the frequency in which the subconscious deploys this method.

Many people say that you have to stop making excuses. This would be tough since it's a subconscious behavior. Like everything else, when life starts to take a positive turn, excuses are going to start disappearing.

ꕤ

STOOPING

One of the versions of excuses I find most fascinating is when people commit hurtful acts and justify it by pointing out that the victim did the same to them. Surely, if he did it to me, isn't it only fair that I do it back? Yes, if you like to be miserable, then that would be the right thing to do.

Remember, we are somehow involved in whatever act is done to us. I'm not saying you deserved it or that you are responsible for it. However, you are a part of the equation. What was done is done; your choice is how things will go in the future. Your choice is to observe your reaction and decide if it will get you where you want to be.

You can look at the time after something hurtful was done to you as a good example of a metaphor of the fork in the road. While we will look at it more closely later on, here's a sneak peek. In a situation where someone hurt you, there's an apparent choice you can make: take the easy out, do the satisfying thing, and hurt back, or be big, forgive, and let it go.

We have to remember that life is a closed loop. We can't do to others without the same energy coming back in some form. Getting someone else back can only lead to more pain, frustration, and more hurtful things being done to us. There's no way around it.

Flipping the story on its head may also shine some light about how events happen in our lives. Here's the reverse version: when something happened to you that brings on revengeful emotions, the resulting emotions are actually the purpose of the entire episode. Somewhere, we all need to feel different emotions at various times. Your need to feel this flavor of emotion matured, and like the need for a cigarette, your subconscious took over and either created the situation that will make it happen or found a situation and reacted in that way.

I know it may seem improbable, but when emotions are concerned, the subconscious has a mighty impact on how we feel and think. It can easily turn a relaxed, sane grown-up into a frustrated and angry person who is so convinced that he or she is right that no argument can change that.

If we have morals that we hold in high regard, and we want to set an example for our peers or children, why would the lesser actions of a lesser person induce us also to act as a lesser person? If anything, another person's lesser acts can serve as a reminder about what not to do and how not to act.

PRIDE

Being proud, as in the opposite of ashamed, is generally considered to be a good thing. Pride is the good feeling we have when others acknowledge us and respect something we did.

But a part of pride is being identified with a life situation, and identification can lead to pain. Can pride be an ingredient of a good life? Let's try to reconcile the two sides.

Much like being satisfied after a period of being hungry, pride is a stepping-stone. If you were hungry for a while and finally got to eat until you were satisfied, you would be so happy that you would want to tell everyone. You would probably be so relieved about eating that you would have your head in the clouds for about a day or two. After that, you would move on. You may still not take not being hungry for granted, but you will also not be the guy who's no longer hungry forever.

The same is true with pride. You may have a life situation that makes you feel good about yourself. Say you're a Marine, you go to a certain school, you are an American, you are a dad of four fantastic children who are good at baseball, or whatever. Being swept with pride once in a while is a good feeling. It is more a joyful sort of pride. Things can get messy when you are so identified with the subject of your pride that it becomes a part of who you are. In a way, you become first the thing and then just a person. You become an American or a Marine instead of a person who has an American citizenship or a person who has a job with the Marines.

There are several scenarios where being overly identified with a life situation can bring pain. To start, that reality can end. If that happens, the ego can take a huge blow, because it used to identify itself with something we considered great.

Another, more severe aspect is that identifying too strongly with a feature of our reality is a bit like walking around with a flag soaked in gasoline, daring people to burn it. It's not so much that someone is going to burn the flag, maybe in the form of pointing out something negative about the thing we are proud of, but more in the constant internal defense position we are stuck in. With pride comes the constant need to monitor the borders and look for any sign that someone out there looks down at our point of pride. This aspect is so much a part of pride that the stress it adds can be undetectable. This stress, however, can be a part of keeping us out of the flow. The internal resistance caused by overexposure to pride can be part of the reason things are not going as we wish they would.

The ego also uses pride as a mask. Why else would the mind need something in our lives to point to and say, "See, we're this, so we're great!" unless it has something it wants to hide from us?

It could also be that you belong to a group that has some social stigma attached to it, such as gay, Native American, Jewish, etc. The external pressure of having people look down or deplore your group caused members to strengthen the pride aspect of the group. We can look at this in two ways. First, there's obviously the oppression aspect. Until fairly recently, you could not be openly gay and serve in the military. There are clubs, institutions, and companies that, while not being openly discriminatory, do discriminate against women, blacks, and other groups. Unless you tie yourself to the mission of abolishing discrimination, there's not much you can do personally fix this.

The other aspect is simply how we feel about it when it is a group you belong to. For example, if you are a part of a minority, do you live under the cloud that, hypothetically, there are people who would not accept you for who you are?

For example, I am Jewish. I never wore a yarmulke or went to synagogue, but Judaism is not something that comes off with soap and water. I am not proud to be Jewish but I am not ashamed of it. Being Jewish is just something I am, like being male, having some Hungarian ancestry, and living in New England. I have no problem with the fact that around the world there must be millions of people who would hate me because I am Jewish. Once, long time ago, I went to the dentist, and as I sat there with my mouth wide open, he asked me why I lived in Providence. He proceeded to tell me that I should move to New York because the Jews control the financial center over there. I got back home, and my wife and I had a good laugh. If I had identified myself with being Jewish, or if it were a subject of pride in my life, this statement would have reminded me that many people have awful stereotypes for Jews, and I would have gotten upset. That event would not have been the worst, though. Worse would be walking around in a defensive position, ready to be attacked for who you are. If you are just yourself, that can never happen.

We have to separate the practical aspect of our minority status from the emotional aspect. We have to realize that most of it is a focus on hypothetical people who don't even know you and possibly don't know about you.

When we meet people, regardless of their personal traits, such as ethnicity, sexual orientation, or gender, we can see right away how much they identify with being that thing. I prefer first to be a person. After that, attach to it all the other things that I am, such as marital status, age, ethnicity, sex, etc. If people want to call me a Jew Bagel, middle class, or whatever it is, good or bad, it is their problem, not mine.

ᘎ•ᘏ

WHAT IF…

A fun way to engage in mental masturbation is to drift into the amazing, almost real fantasy about what could have been. It's incredible how life seems to be a collection of almost-events, each little twist in any way would make our situations a hundred times better than what it ended up being. Or better yet, things could have almost been horrible, which means that something horrible is always around the corner.

If only I looked in the paper that day…what if I just answered the phone…if the chicken had just stopped at the bank before crossing the road…

Would it be too harsh to say that what-if scenarios, when used in a regretful way (should and could have been better), are pointless?

In the universe, there is no such thing as *what-ifs*. There are no other scenarios other than exactly what happened. What happened, as it affected our lives, fits our lives, and happened to match our beliefs. It may have the appearance of a random event, but it is not. Meaningful events, good and bad, happen to align our lives with what we believe they can be.

There is, however, one way in which we can use what-if scenarios to our advantage. This is a trick my wife uses to calm anxiety. When there's a situation or potential outcome that causes her stress, she imagines the absolute worst-case scenario actually happening, and she imagines that even that would not be all that bad. This controlled version of what-if works well because you are the one summoning it to reduce anxiety, rather than your ego using it to raise anxiety.

꧁◆꧂

REGRET

Regret is a particularly exciting variety of the what-if family of scenarios. It is especially horrible when we are prone to blame ourselves for various things, and feelings of regret can do a number on us. Once the idea that we just narrowly messed up by one small misstep takes hold, it can be devastating.

If you didn't get this from the previous section, then it's a good thing to repeat: nothing you could have done differently would have changed anything. What-if is a cruel self-delusion. Nothing in your life so far could happen any other way. Events in your life are a result of more than just coincidence, and there was no possibility of you acting in any way other than the way you acted. Now, if you are suffering from chronic regret, please know that it is a self-perpetuating, habitual thought pattern whose sole purpose is to drag you down.

From this point on, whenever you are tormented by thoughts that you have messed up your life by making this or that wrong move, please observe those thoughts and know that their role is to keep you from moving on. They have no other purpose. They are a part of a defense mechanism gone very wrong. Observe them and let them go.

We can deploy the magic question trick here as well. When attacked with regretful feelings, ask yourself, *is there anything I can do to change what happened?* If the answer is no, then just drop it.

ↀ✦ↀ

URGENCY

In this section, we will look at the role urgency plays in our lives. Having a sense of urgency, the sense that we have to do something in a rush and that nothing else really matters, is most likely habitual and not totally justified.

In life, a sense of urgency is rarely actually justified. However, many times we have the feeling of having to act at once and having no time to think clearly about what we have to do. It's as if the subconscious puts us in sort of a personal state of emergency. What is really happening has very little to do with the situation or what needs to be done. After all, I bet that no one is counting on you to defuse a bomb in a busy mall, negotiate a peace treaty in Africa, or save people trapped in a house fire. When we feel we are in "urgency mode," we need to observe these times. When we feel this (temporarily) hysterical outlook, where we have to achieve something fast and disregard people around us, we need to become present. It will be tough to change our actions at that point, but we should just be aware of them. Later, look back to determine the cause of that sense of urgency. It's likely to fall in one of two categories: either the same result could have been achieved calmly, or somehow, the subconscious had a hand in why urgency was required.

By "you," I mean your subconscious, of course. If urgency happens to be in your repertoire of habitual emotions, then your subconscious will always find reasons to bring that emotion about.

Remember, there are very few times in our normal lives where urgency is truly needed.

When urgency is truly needed, when it's a matter of life and death, the subconscious will take over anyway and lead the way. You will have a very small part in it, so there's no real way to plan for it and no reason to worry about it.

When urgency happens to be a habitual emotion, the subconscious will always find reasons to bring that emotion about. Feeling a chronic lack of time is in everyday situations is habitual. Life can be set up so that we are constantly in a rush and have no time to stop and take a breath. We are stressed and stressing out everyone around us.

Here's an idea to take in: *there is always time to do anything we need, comfortably.* Feeling rushed or time-stressed is a core belief that brings on those stressful feelings. Since those beliefs were most likely held for a while, the subconscious has created many situations that allow us to plunge into the comfort of the *I-have-no-time* mode. In reality, taking our time can always get better results and not leave us with a bad feeling.

ℰ𝒪◆𝒞𝒮

WASTING TIME

The subconscious likes to toy with us by using time. We are so obsessed with the efficient use of our time that we forget just to be. We will be much happier without the idea of wasting time.

Look at the idea of time waste a bit closer so that we can maybe take some of the sting out of it. But why bother? We waste time here and there, we get annoyed, and everything gets back to normal, right?

Not so.

We cannot just disregard little annoyances in life, because they are a pointer to bigger issues that haunt us. Any time the ego tells us that something in our lives is not as it should be and that thought causes anxiety, that anxiety is tied on the other side to pain. Going through the paces of being annoyed, complaining, and so on only ensures that we will get more of the same. When we want change, we need to look at those little things that annoy us, that get us off-kilter, and figuring out fresh ways to look at them.

Now back to our subject matter.

We're usually annoyed with wasting time when we believe we are in the process of wasting time or just finished some activity deemed a waste of time. By that time, however, it is already too late! It is done. That thing we believe is time we should have back to use for whatever better things we would have done with it is gone forever. We are that much closer to our eventual demise with nothing to show for the past four minutes, three hours, or day of our lives. What a waste.

Obviously, this is a dramatization with a tinge of cynicism, but it can help put things in perspective. Why is wasting time so bad?

We learn very early in life that time is money, which makes wasting time a typical trigger for anxiety and frustration. Also, since we live such busy lives, any amount of time we spend in a way we deem unproductive or not fun makes us feel that our personal time was shortened.

But what we forget is that how we feel—not what we do—makes up the quality of life. This means that since the time we spent is already "wasted," feeling annoyed about it is wasting even more time and energy!

Also, remember that putting an emotional weight behind things in life is a sure way to invite them to come back again.

❧•☙

WAITING

Other aspects of expectation—time wasting and the kitchen timer effect—can be experienced whenever we are caught having to do some unexpected waiting. These times are a great opportunity to observe our automatic reactions and question them. Two specific such events we often experience in our daily lives are at line in the grocery store and being stuck in traffic.

Unless you're the secretary of state on your way to Middle East peace talks or a fireman having to put out an ongoing fire right after buying something at the store, then you have plenty of time. Really, the additional two minutes you'll have to wait will not make any difference in your life or anyone else's. If they do make a difference, you are one in a million, your life is wound far too tightly, or, most likely, you are far too important in your own mind.

When we find ourselves stuck in a situation where we have to do more waiting than intended, ask this question right away: Is there something I can do right now to make the situation better for me? Change lanes, change checkout lines, make a call, etc. If yes, do it. Since there is most likely nothing to do, I have something for you: practice patience.

That's right. Acting aggravated at how slow the line is going has no effect on the speed of the line, and it only makes you and the rest of the shoppers less able to enjoy their time.

This is true whenever we are randomly annoyed with something. It is just that driving and shopping are classic, repeatable, and universal examples, so it is easy to catch yourself in the act. Every time you catch yourself getting annoyed while standing in line, just yell, "Could people move a little faster, I have a world to save!" This should put things in perspective.

Realize that the path to a happier, less anxious life goes through those little habitual annoyed reactions. Observe them and they will slowly weaken. You will possibly still end up waiting in line and stuck in traffic just as much, but your improved reaction and more positive outlook on the opportunity to just hang out in the car or chat with the people around you in the store rather than being upset will make your now better and therefore your life better. As Eckhart Tolle said in The Power of Now, "I wasn't waiting. I was just enjoying myself." I love this guy!

჻ ◆ ჻

FIGHT

There is the fight against cancer, the war against drugs, and fights against obesity, hunger, terror, and on and on. It seems that wherever we turn, we are fighting for something we believe in. Being in some sort of a resistance, such as a fight or a war, is not confined to the streets of Afghanistan. It is going on around us all the time. In fact, the fight is not around us, but rather inside of us.

Since you have been so good and read that far, I want to tell you what I think about fighting. When we put a strong emotional charge behind our beliefs and intentions, we fuel them and make more of the same come our way. To our point, fighting anything serves the opposite purpose we intended.

Fighting for something is different, although I prefer work for it rather than fight for it. Putting our energy behind something we want more of is a good thing.

The contradiction occurs when the dominating aspect of our effort is what we want to get rid of. Fighting against things like disease, drugs, or war—no matter what it is—we can't get rid of it by fighting against it. It's like putting out fire with fuel.

I am not going to get into why we feel the urge to fight things. I do not know why the slogan Join the Fight Against Cancer brings millions in donations and volunteers, but Join Us in Allowing Wellness with Our Love would draw a handful of penniless hippies. But the sad fact is that the second one, as pathetic as it may sound, is a much more effective approach.

Anything that causes us discomfort, such as war, disease, violence, and hunger, can only be amplified by our angry calls to end it. The only choice we can make to get what we want is to love and allow. It may seem like a catch-22: there are things that we do not want, but resisting them makes them stronger. It may seem hopeless, but there are other ways.

Remember the flow from earlier? The flow is the stream of goodness in life that we all have access to. We can't be in the flow when we resist, resent, or fight. We can be in the flow when we allow, when we are grateful, and when we love.

Am I really suggesting here that you should love your cancer? Should we really allow drugs? First, what we are doing now is obviously not working. The rate of preventable disease and substance abuse are far too high. I'm not suggesting that you replace your doctor with a love letter to your tumor, but to stop hating your tumor while your doctors are working on it is an amazing thing you can do right away. No matter what makes our lives miserable, resisting it, hating it, complaining about it, or becoming its victim does not help to make it go away. It does the opposite.

This is your life, and you are on a journey on your own. You may have friends and family, but it is up to you to find what is not working. Whatever is not working is not outside and is not random. It starts and ends with you.

REVENGE

Ah, the joy of planning to get back at someone. They screwed you over, and you are going to show them who is the boss.

Unfortunately, this is yet another rowing motion in the wrong direction. When the ego is constantly itching to push us in that direction, it is because the ego is getting us to feel the way we are used to feeling. If someone did something to you that made you feel bad, the only way to keep the bad feeling going is to get them back somehow. They brought it on themselves, but you also brought it on yourself.

The first thing you're doing in this scenario is avoiding responsibility. The test is simple: if it's a part of our lives, especially a part that makes us feel bad, we have a part in it. It may be uncomfortable, but when I blame someone else, I am not resolving anything. The path that leads to making things in life better passes through taking complete ownership of our lives and everything in it. Now, if we own everything, why would we want to make it worse by taking revenge, even in a small way?

Another side effect of revenge is that we are inviting the other person to make our lives even worse. If you took revenge on them, they are much more likely to continue the back and forth and bring even more misery to your reality. Are you somehow looking for them to be the big person and stop?

On a cosmic scale, when we plan and take revenge, we also tint the entire universe with a tiny bit of negativity. Not a lot, but when many people add a bit of negativity to the collective pot, it can amount to a lot.

Revenge is one of those emotions that the ego is keen on, and the intensity with which it urges us to partake in it can be haunting. When revenge is your thing, thoughts of why, when, and how to get someone back are going to torment you until you take action. It's a tough cycle to end, and it starts with knowing that it is a part of why your life sucks sometimes.

❧•☙

EMBARRASSMENT

I feel for my kids. Before we attend events with their friends, they have to sit me down and give me a stern talking-to about not doing anything embarrassing. They are kids, however, and despite my best effort, something slips, and they get embarrassed.

For grown-ups, however, embarrassment can be an entirely different thing.

Of course, the occasional moment when you wish the earth would swallow you is unavoidable. The chronic embarrassment episodes are what we have to watch for.

Embarrassment and shame are some of the worst emotions to have. They can drag us down and make us feel so unworthy, we'd rather not live.

Those emotions always come with a perfect excuse. After all, it's the event that triggered the emotion that causes us to feel what we feel, right? Can we really blame ourselves for feeling ashamed or embarrassed? We can, and it is possible that at times we do, but it does not do any good.

The triggering event is a cosmic cover-up for the real reason we feel that way. The real reason is simply that we need to feel that way. Any negative emotion we feel on a regular basis is a habitual rather than a legitimate reaction to an event. The mind needs to get that specific emotion going, like a drug, and it will find the excuse to make it happen. So what is there to do?

We start by understanding on an intellectual level that shame and embarrassment are almost never justified emotions. We need to realize that even though we can't really control what we are being hit with emotionally, we can be aware and present. The place where we fall hard is in identifying and agreeing with the nonsense the subconscious throws in our way—the stuff intended to convince us that the negative emotions that sweep us are justified and unavoidable.

The second step is awareness, either while we're in the middle of feeling the embarrassment or as soon after it as possible. In the eye of the storm, it can be rather difficult to observe what is happening to us, but we have to take that step.

The third step is letting go. As we are bombarded by an assault on our emotions, we have to let go of the focus on shame that those emotions come with. Understand that shame is one of the lowest emotions on the scale of our awareness. Being hit often with the sense that your very existence is a reason to want to hide is very difficult to snap out of.

⁂

AVOIDING PEOPLE

Who doesn't have someone they need to avoid? Someone you dated, someone you worked with, an ex-friend, etc. When you live in New York City, which I don't, avoiding people must be easy. You simply don't make an effort to see them, and they just disappear in the crowd. For the rest of us, a simple trip to the grocery store can become an unwanted social event where we do not know who we are going to run into. If there's someone special we are trying to avoid, we have to be on the lookout and resort to evasive maneuvers when necessary.

But is it necessary, and what are the repercussions, if any?

I can't speak for anyone else, but to me, having to avoid people is not the way I like to live. Believe me, there were plenty of people in my life that I prefer to never see again. As you know, however, this is exactly when life throws them right in your face. I know that awful cowering feeling of knowing they saw you and pretending you didn't see them. I decided not to deal with that type of nonsense. I no longer avoid anyone. This is my world, and if anyone has a reason to avoid me, it's their thing. Anyone I chose to avoid before, if I see them, I just go and say hi. No hiding, no resenting—just stepping up.

I realized that avoiding people had a negative effect on my life, and that it could be corrected rather easily by simply strapping on a pair and making swift contact. My intent was not to make anyone uncomfortable, but to get it over with and move on. This beats accumulating baggage any day!

ꕤ•ꕤ

JUDGING PEOPLE

One of the first things people learn when they want to become better people is to not judge others. Ironically, some people rush to judge anyone else who judges shortly after that realization. They say, "Hey, don't say that! It's judgmental!"

It's perfectly acceptable to not want to judge, but it is more difficult than you think. Judging people's actions, on the other hand, is a funny thing.

Let's look at the following simple scenario: you're driving down the open road, and a really annoying driver is in front of you. That driver drives a bit slowly, but you can't seem to pass him, which gets you a bit upset. After a block or so, you see the New Driver sign through the car's rear window. Ha! He's a new driver. Your annoyance dissipates, and the "teacher" in you wakes up and says, "Take your time" with a smile. So one piece of information about a complete stranger turned you from being an annoyed jerk into feeling just dandy. My question is, why be upset in the first place? Being upset is, well, being upset. It doesn't feel good. Instead, understand that there's a choice to quietly observe yourself getting upset, and say, "Here I am getting upset about nothing." Then you do not get any further upset.

Let's look at a different judgment scenario. Say you read the paper, and there's a story about this guy that robbed a bank. You read it and judge that person negatively. You read on and discover that the bank has foreclosed on his home. Now you judge the bank, all banks, and the institution of banking, and the guy is off the hook. You read on and see that this is the fifth foreclosure this guy had, and he's a chronic debtor. Arrgh...those people! The guy is in the doghouse again, and so on and so forth.

Even if you read that robber's entire unabridged biography, you will still only have a snippet of information about him that will allow you accurately to decide if he is the good guy or the bad guy. People should be held responsible for anything in their lives, but unless they are the ones holding themselves responsible, there's no point.

Judging others has one perpetrator: the ego. Among other things, it is trying to mask the uncomfortable things we should be taking responsibility for. As long as our attention is on other people's faults, the ego knows we won't look at ourselves. Besides having no business judging others, any difference such judgment makes in another person's life—and yours—is only negative.

As we saw at the start, the most fun we have judging people is, ironically, after one gets the idea that judging is a bad idea. Of course, the ego instantly shifts the gaze from an internal examination to judgment of others. As soon as we perceive that they are biting the forbidden fruit of judgment and we are their only hope for salvation, we let them have it. Our initial reaction is to judge everyone else for their judging.

This, of course, does nothing good. Why? Because as much as it is fun to figure out what other people are doing wrong, it only puts them on the defensive and hides the painful truth from us: we are the judgmental ones. Ouch!

So, the next time you manage to see through your ego's veil and notice yourself cast judgment on someone else, contemplate this: What aspect of my own life is my ego trying to mask by pointing out another person's issues?

JUDGMENTAL LISTENING

As we listen to another person during a conversation, we automatically form an opinion about what they are saying. In other words, we are judging it. This judgment happens instantly, and unless we pay attention, this judgment can be seen in our expressions, body language, and response.

While it can make for a more interesting and dramatic conversation and is an opportunity to voice an opinion, expressing judgment also has a down side.

When someone shares an opinion with you in a conversation, a part of them is always on guard for your reaction. Whether you agree with them or not, you fulfill a function that fills a need in them. That need, however, is the ego's need. Their ego will either try to get a negative reaction or an agreement, but it will always be alert to see what's coming.

When you offer your opinion in your response, you make the conversation more engaging and fun, which is a good purpose. When a conversation is more contentious, your opinion might influence the conversation in an unintended direction that may not be constructive.

Consider an example that can clarify this type of situation. You are in an argument, meaning that at least you seem to want the other side over to your side. You want them to see your point of view and if not agreeing with it, at least considering it.

You already know that people take a long time to form opinions and hardly ever change them drastically. They do, but not often. A person's beliefs are a block of ice that may come crashing down one day, but most likely, the ice melts away bit by bit. All we can hope for is to help that melting process move along.

When we throw our opinions in someone's face, we inadvertently activate their defenses, or, in other words, they become defensive. This defensiveness may show itself in many forms: lash back, argue back, get offended, or just appear completely unaffected. But they almost certainly have just become less likely to hear what we have to say. We caused them to shut down to our point of view, which was not our intent and goes against our goal. I do that once in a while, for fun, but I realize it has no positive benefit to the situation or the world other than giving myself some momentary satisfaction of beating someone in an argument.

Once we realize that (1) we cannot change someone's mind and turn it 180 degrees to see things the way we do and (2) their opinion does not change who we are, we can listen to them without judgment—without thinking that we are right and they are wrong and without having all the "facts" they are missing run through our heads. When we do that, something very special happens. The other person, probably for the first time in a long time, can actually hear himself or herself.

As we know from earlier in the book, observation is a powerful tool. We can't make other people observe themselves, but we can allow them to and give them the space.

EGO LISTENING

When we have a conversation, the ego usually takes over, listens, and argues for us. It believes that a conversation takes far too much responsibility to allow us to deal with it. After all, the ego is attached to our opinions.

Our opinion and point of view make up a large part of who we believe we are. Left wing, right wing, Christian, Muslim, Jewish, vegetarian, gay, etc.—no matter what our convictions are, we can sometimes carry them like a flag. We identify with them, and it appears that people around us expect us to hold the party line.

When having an argument or heated discussion, we are actually fighting to uphold that position. Actually, the ego specifically has an interest in maintaining our public view a certain way. The ego is not aware of or interested in anyone's well-being or the common good. That's what makes the ego a horrible listener. Our egos take everything heard in a discussion and automatically light a fire to heat things up. There is very little listening going on.

Our job is to break that and realize and observe our need to appear a certain way to the outside. The next time you argue anything, make an effort to really listen. Find as many similarities as you can with the person you're conversing with. In your mind, find them as right as possible. Both of you will gain much more from the experience.

Another aspect of listening is responsible for negative aspects of our reality: being right.

BEING RIGHT

How do you write a short section about a subject that can have entire books dedicated to it? The need to be right, rivaled only by our need to not be at fault, is an odd impulse that can transform intelligent people into complete idiots in a matter of seconds.

Being right and having everyone know we are right, is without a doubt one of the ego's favorite things to do. It is also our greatest downfall.

For some reason, it is such an important thing that while arguing with someone about which one of you is right, nothing else seems to matter. It's as if we're hit with a spell, and are being forced to squabble the completely irrelevant point of who's right.

In any argument, there are a few aspects. The subject matter, of course, is most important. Then, equally as important but different is how people in the conversation feel. Somewhere near the bottom of the list, at the least important side, is which person is right. Yet we will still go to the ends of the earth to argue our case, far beyond the point where a part of us realized that we lost.

The funny thing is, when we truly are right, we don't have a burning need to have others know it. Truly being right is a quiet sensation of knowing that does not have to be made public. When you have a good point, you can wait patiently to state it, and having others know you are right doesn't seem to matter.

Another aspect of being right is getting annoyed when someone shares a fact we already know. C'mon, give the poor guy the satisfaction! People usually tell us things because it is fun to share a fact and get a reaction, so don't be a wet blanket.

Seriously, this is not the point. The point is to observe yourself in those situations so that you can be in the moment when your ego usually takes over and makes a total fool out of you.

What's good about being right is that the irony is obvious, making it easy to see the disparity between how we behave and how we know we should behave. The inherited egotistical nature of throwing the important purpose of the conversation under the bus just to appear smart is so glaring that it can give us an impetus to catch ourselves in the act next time it happens.

It's important to catch ourselves because when the ego takes over doing stupid stuff, it makes sure that we are not completely aware to tell it to shut up. The ego has gotten used to being able to do whatever it wants without interruption. When we wake up, catch it in the act, and observe it as it wreaks havoc, we make it difficult for it to operate. Its grip on our lives is weakened.

You may wonder what the problem is with letting people know you are right. Well, nothing is inherently wrong with people knowing. But if you are right once, it won't matter anyway, because you will appear as being wrong most of the time. If you are right a lot of the time and make smart points, people will know anyway, consider you smart, and value your opinion. Isn't that the point? Being your own agent and spreading the word about your own rightness makes you sound dumb.

There is another, more important reason to catch the ego. Whenever we let the ego take over a conversation, the eventual outcome is always unpleasant. There's pain tied to the other end of anything the ego does. Watch it happen, observe it, and talk yourself through making being right less of a priority.

Here's a fun thing to try: the next time you find yourself arguing any point whatsoever, argue a bit and then just admit defeat!

Just slowly say something like, "You know what? This was a good point. I think you just might be right on this one." You'll notice that the world didn't end and you will gain someone's trust and make them really happy. Maybe, most of all, you will give your own pesky ego something to think about.

ဆ◆ဆ

THE TRUTH

Growing attached to being the truth-bearer for the universe is another common dysfunction. Going past the slightly annoying aspects of being right, people who hold on to the truth of human kind are usually closer to the edge than you or I.

Much like being right, when we are aware of some genuine piece of truth, we don't feel the need to demean anyone who doesn't share that truth.

But if we are stuck in the delusion that we are the holders of truth and justice and are convinced that we are somehow better than those who don't see things our way, we have some serious things to consider. That sense of holding the torch of truth is a part of a circle of pain in our lives. It may be very difficult, but questioning our hold on "truth" is a good place to start.

ဆ◆ဆ

GOSSIP

Few activities are as fun as talking about other people when they are not there. Ah, how slowly releasing our grasp on juicy information fills us with invincibility. We can pretty much say anything we want to a crowd of eager listeners, who are all looking forward to when they will get to share the juicy news with their own clique.

Gossip is so much fun to do that it makes us forget about good taste, about the golden rule, about the harm we are causing and the poison we are spreading.

The controlled dispensing of information about people we know has always been a way to gain a sense of power, even if only for a moment. There's something about that feeling of telling a story that shows someone in a bad light. Timing the information just right, sharing with the right group of people, and knowing how to pepper the story is nothing short of art.

So is gossip bad? Like with anything else, it is all a matter of moderation and intention.

If we are looking to become more enlightened and to sweep all traces of bad karma from life, then we should cease gossiping cold turkey. On the other hand, occasionally discussing aspects of someone else's life is unavoidable and may be harmless.

When we rely on gossiping to give ourselves a sense of worth or an ego boost, we may have a problem. Gossip is no doubt the ego's work. The type of enjoyment it gives is in line with other mental addictions. Therefore, overdoing it, looking forward to it, and gaining a good sensation from it is not healthy. As always, relying on the ego to make us feel good always comes with a steep price.

You may have a gossip problem if you ask yourself if you have a gossip problem, and your answer is either, "Possibly" or "Absolutely not an option!"

ꕥ•ꕥ

EXCLUSIVITY

Our egos love identifying with exclusive things: parties, clubs, meetings, invitations, credit cards, etc. The great thing about things that are exclusive is not the thing itself, but that other people don't get to have or do them.

Hold on. Rewind. I need to hear myself say it again, because the first time it sounded just too dumb to be real. Here goes: we love exclusive things because it separates us from other people we deem less worthy. Yup—sounds just as strange. Must be something the ego likes to strokes itself with.

Groucho Marx said it best, "I do not care to belong to a club that accepts people like me as members."

The road paved with enjoying exclusivity has a single destination: pain. Thriving on the belief that others are not worthy of the same things that we are or that we are in any way better off than someone who does not belong to our club can only bring temporary satisfaction. Once we belong to that proverbial club, we spend time drenched in the satisfaction the status is giving us, but, soon enough, the ego is unhappy again. The separation created between you and most of humanity will not be enough, and the ego will want to belong to an even more exclusive group inside that group you just joined. This unsustainable process has the typical ego-operated mechanics of never being quite satisfied and wanting more every time you enter a new stage. Eventually, the entire system implodes over you.

Accepting satisfaction from the ego is like taking out a loan from a loan shark: the terms are never as sweet as they seem to be when you signed the deal.

But the ego's need for exclusivity doesn't end there. The concept of exclusivity, in a way, drives our entire economy. Think about the concept of owning gold. You can buy an ounce of it for a whole lot more than you would spend for an ounce of silver, for example. This is because it is rarer, and therefore more exclusive and more desirable. In fact, our entire economy is based on the relatively low availability of gold, and our desire to own things that are not easy to own. This is true for food as well. For example, lobster was considered a poor person's food and was fed to prisoners a hundred or so years ago. Lobster was so plentiful that it was used to fertilize corn. Nowadays, ordering Maine lobster is considered an expensive treat, and in some places, it is reserved for the few that can afford it. So does lobster taste better now than it did a hundred years ago? Of course! Taste is nothing but our minds judging a sensation. Taste can be changed just like any other habit. If you had heard for a while about this amazing "rare and exclusive" treat, when you ate it, your taste would be biased.

Building our sense of self by distinguishing ourselves as better than other people only leads to hurt. The old saying is true: *the best things in life are free*. This is not just a throwaway line we can use and move on with life. When we truly live by this line, we are all enlightened. The best things in life are things that give you true, long-lasting, sustainable joy: someone to love, clean air to breathe, and some raw vegetables. Of course, at this point your mind-set might tell you that simple things are stupid, and that the way to happiness is paved with caring more about material things, acquiring more things other people can't have, and padding your bank account with more zeros. There's nothing wrong with that, but the other side of it just may be an impending emptiness and dissatisfaction.

ℬ•ℭ

BEST THING THAT CAN EVER HAPPEN TO YOU

It's funny how the things people are most anxious about end up being the things that end up drastically changing their lives for the better.

Imagine (or remember, if needed) being dumped by a spouse. It sounds like a horrible thing. We can use that event as a reason for endless complaining and self-pity. But think about what really happened.

First, you were living with a person who felt differently about you than you felt about them. It is a bad thought, but it's also a sobering thought. What happened is that you were not paying attention. How can you not have been paying attention? Usually your spouse doesn't go off for three months, come back, and announce their separation. They are right there with you, most of the time. The reality of your relationship was very different from what you thought it was. As bad as this may have been, it is now over! You are no longer under the delusion that your marriage would last forever while your spouse is either imagining sleeping with someone else or already taking action on that end.

Being awake is much better. Take a hot shower, put on a nice shirt, raise your head up high, and decide that you want a new life where you are actually with someone who wants to be with you.

There is a similar sentiment for being laid off. Imagine your company was looking for the least useful employees to let go of. This is nothing personal, but they did you a huge favor! Why? Were you not waiting for an opportunity to start over? Were you not looking to be able to work more at doing what you loved? Were you not toying with the idea of starting your own business or just freelancing for a while?

You were just handed that opportunity. Stop whining; it will not convince anyone to give you your old job back. Imagine something new and fresh and make it happen.

CHAPTER 17

Money

Nothing is more synonymous with life's problems than money. When we have it, we have problems, and if we don't have it, we have even more problems. Few things in life are tied to our psyche like a ton of bricks, ready to bring us down at every mention, as money is.

I bet if we asked the first hundred people if they would choose right now to always have money or always be happy, they would go with the money. The rationale would be this: *if I have money, I will certainly be happy, so I'll take the money and have both.*

I think many people who have money would find that ironic. Richer people may be happier than you are, or they may not be, but either way, it has nothing to do with money. The reversal of logic is another factor that plays a role in our ability to gain money and keep it. People say *when they have money, they'll be happy.*

A little fact for you: if you have no money and are not happy, and this is what you think, you will never have either. On the other hand, if you are happy—and I mean truly change your life around and let go of the need to have money—then money is going to start coming to you in ways you never imagined.

This can sound a bit problematic. First, if our reality is such that we are lacking money, how in the world can we let go of needing it? We shouldn't need to let go of the physical need for money that we use for food, rent, gas, etc. However, it will not hurt to let go of the emotional meaning money has in our lives.

Money, for the most part, is not even real. Money is bytes on a bank's many computer servers, or, if you don't have a bank account, it's a pile of paper. It is not your kid in the hospital, it's not your arm that you're going to lose, and it's not a nation at war. It is just money.

I know—you work hard, and you earn money that buys things that allow you to live. My idea is not for you to have less of it—quite the opposite: I think having a lot of money is fun. But to have enough money, we have to tweak the way we think and feel about it. We have to change our relationship with money.

As long as money is the cause of negative emotions in our lives, the situation will never change, at least not in the long term. As long as we see our relationship with money as a struggle, it will be. As long as we believe that we have to stretch every dollar and as long as we feel poor, we will be. As long as we keep telling ourselves, and anyone else lucky enough to be listening, all about our money problems, new versions of those money problems will keep finding their way into our lives.

Those statements may appear foreign and unlikely, but how do you explain your situation? Bad economy? Really? I guess you had tons of money in the nineties. Or is it just your bad luck? It is not luck. Isolated events may appear to occur at random, much like grains of sand may appear random when you look at them closely. But when you look back, you can either see a beautiful, purposeful sand castle or a purposeless pile of sand. If you walked on the beach and met someone sitting next to a pile of sand complaining that it's just bad luck that life isn't shaping the sand into the beautiful castle he dreams of, would you feel his pain or wonder why he doesn't just shape it to be what he wants? With money, almost anyone can make a dream castle!

Since most of us learn from a young age that money doesn't grow on trees, that we work all our lives, and that if we are lucky, we have some money at the end, thinking differently about money can be difficult. If you just imagine that there is a different way to view money, that's good enough for now. And if you are ready for the next step, that's even better.

Even though money doesn't grow on trees, it is created and distributed in a similar manner. Money, like all things in our universe, has its own energy signature. Money is also not inherently bad. In fact, being in the flow also means allowing money to come to us. The only difference between attracting money and attracting problems is that most of us are deeply convinced that our current situation is how life is, that this is our reality. Since this is what we believe, this is what our reality looks like. And, as long our families, friends, and newspapers agree with us, we have very little reason to change our beliefs. But how do we know that this is not the way things really are? What can tell us with certainty that there is another way?

We all hear, while drooling with jealousy, these stories about self-made people who started with nothing and were millionaires by the time they turned thirty. Whatever those people do makes them money. They have the "Midas touch." If we asked them whether making money was difficult, they would smile and answer a definitive no. This doesn't mean they don't work hard for it, but it is not a struggle. For some reason, they escaped the hereditary social disease that makes us all believe that money is hard to come by. But if they attract money, and we don't, how can we be like them and start attracting money? We can't. We can't be like them, but we also don't need to. You have to do nothing in order to start attracting money!

Money is like sunshine: it constantly flies all over the place in all directions. It is like energy, being constantly made and spent, exchanging hands, and is seen as cash, checks, or mostly as electrical pulses flying between computers around the world. So why does more of it pass through other people than through you? Very simple: wealthy people allow money to come to them.

Believing that you we lack, and being anxious about that lack blocks the natural flow of anything in the universe. This is true for love and anything else that can be put on the proverbial how-much-of-it-do-I-have scale. If our reality is that we lack money, and we put a negative emotional weight on it, we are blocking the natural flow of money that otherwise we would be a part of.

This can be very confusing, and if you do buy into this idea, the first thought you have may be that it is up to you to be in the flow, allow more in, etc., but you may have little to no idea as to how to accomplish it.

Some will make you believe that it is all at your fingertips, and all you have to do is imagine it, and it will come. This is partially true, but the missing part is essential. It is a bit like driving on the highway and seeing a restaurant from your car window. You're hungry, and there's the food, so close, but there's no apparent way to get to it. What can make this more annoying is that you know that the instructions are somewhere in your car, but you just can't find them.

The problem with flow-blockers is that some are manifested in the form of negative actions or self-talk, and some are deeper and take shape subconsciously.

The good thing is that there are plenty of ways in which we are in the flow. There are many examples we can use to show us that life is effortless and getting what we want with very little effort is possible. Those other aspects of life work on the same principle as money, and we can draw inspiration from them. For example, making money is much like growing a plant on your porch, getting in your car and driving to the park, or making a peanut butter and jelly sandwich. The difference is not the objective, but rather our beliefs and emotional connections.

MONEY DOESN'T GROW ON TREES

True, but as we worked out earlier, it works in a similar way. If we don't block the tree from growing apples, new ones will grow every season. As long as the tree has the right conditions, we'll need to do very little to pick the fruit.

Of course, if we visited the local orchard, got excited, and bought a sapling, we might kill it because growing a tree does require some work, and we have some learning to do.

The same is true for money. Once the conditions for growing money are right, money just grows. It keeps on coming and going, like apples, but we always have enough of it. Unlike an apple tree, though, the conditions for growing money are within us. They are our core beliefs, which we feed with our thoughts, actions, and reactions.

Now let's say that you're an experienced tree grower, or you get the idea of growing a tree and believe you can do it. How can you apply the same principles toward making money?

A tree must be planted in fertile ground to grow. Planting a sapling in concrete or gravel will just not work. That fertile ground for money in our lives is our belief that it can happen. Don't fool yourself, though: we are only aware of a small fraction of our core beliefs. We may need to do some serious work to uncover some of them and lay a fresh layer of new beliefs in their stead. Those beliefs can be deeply rooted, and may take some time to understand and replace.

My favorite method of laying fertile ground for growing money is visualization. Seeing ourselves how we want to be is powerful, but it also takes practice and some dedication. Believe me, if it took more than a little dedication, I would not have done it. I have the attention span of a squirrel.

Visualization is powerful because as we see things in our minds, they start to manifest in reality. This takes some time, but it always starts with a vision. As soon as we decide to visualize, say, being financially independent, the ego starts with creeping doubts, making vision difficult. The ego is an expert in coming up with reasons why something can't happen. We start getting caught on details, while the ego, believing that it has the tools to make this happen, starts to bombard us with potential obstacles.

Settle down, release those blocking thoughts as they come, and just allow yourself to dream. It may feel stupid or delusional, but it is not. It is the most powerful creation tool you have for shaping your reality.

MAKING MONEY AND SPENDING IT

It seems reasonable that the money we have is a factor of the money we make and the money we spend or save. While mathematically it works that way, the mechanism that makes it happen is not under our control. Don't get me wrong: we set the direction and the agenda, but we still control nothing.

Take my situation right now. I am on a train to New York City. I could have gone on any other train or gotten off at any other station. I could also stay on this train all the way to Washington. But no; I set my destination at New York, and that is where I will get off. While this is fully up to me, I am not aware how this is happening, and I can't control any of it. I can't make the train go faster or slower, make the correct turn, or even know whether it's making the right turns. The same goes for you and money. You set the direction with your thoughts and beliefs, and your subconscious is responsible for executing it. All you can really do is experience it. You can make heroic attempts to command the operation and control it, but the fruit of your efforts will either be short-lived or affect your situation negatively.

Controlling how you make and spend money is like me controlling the train going to New York. If I tried, the best scenario is that I'd find myself restrained to my seat. At worst, I'd be asked to get off at the nearest station. Instead, I am just sitting, enjoying the view, and getting some writing done.

This scenario is also true for writing this book: I imagined it, and now it is as if it's writing itself. I am sitting and words are being spilled onto my computer. I know it is coming from somewhere in me, but I am certainly not in control of the process.

Would You Still Have the Money Now?

A fun question we like to ask once in a while is if you didn't spend that money in the past, would you still have that money in the bank today?

The answer is a resounding no. First, you know my take on what-ifs; they are a delusion. Regardless, the amount of money we have is not a result of what we make and spend. The opposite is true. Making and spending money is a tool the subconscious uses to align our financial situation with our beliefs. The money we have is not the mathematical result of random subtraction and addition. There is a pattern and a purpose.

Once we figure out the method we use to tell the subconscious to block money, we may be able to stop and allow more money in. Very much like, earlier on the train, I discovered that even if I ended up breaking into the conductor's car and started pressing random buttons, it wouldn't get me any closer to New York, but quite the opposite.

BILLS

Gauging our reactions to bills as they reliably come from various sources can be a fun experiment in discovering how we view money. Somehow, most of us manage to be stressed by bills. If you think about it for a minute, you will also realize that if this is not the dumbest thing we do, it is certainly "up there" on the list.

We usually start our affair with bills when we move into our own place—going off to college, work, etc. Mom and Dad are no longer there, and we are rather unprepared to deal with all that life is ready to dump on us.

At first, it's the phone and electric bills. Then it's cable, insurance of some kind, and so on from there. Since we all have bills, and most of us have similar reactions to them, they can make a great platform for self-observation.

Let's first agree on some basic things. First, being upset or anxious about bills is plain dumb. Most of those bills come every month, and all they ask is that we fulfill commitments we made. The other end is that we get to enjoy the benefits of the services provided all month long. We *can* live with a fraction of the monthly bills we get now; it's just that electricity and phone are too darn exciting to live without.

The total amount of the bills we get is irrelevant to our financial situations. Monthly expenses, like any other money exchange we make, are used to equalize our situations and leave us with a certain amount of money, which in turn leaves us with a specific feeling.

It's not so much that the subconscious monitors our money, because all it cares about is making us feel a certain way. Bills work well since we get our fix of anxiety, despair, annoyance, or whatever it is you're used to feeling when we get bills on a regular basis.

Now that we agree that stressing out about bills is pointless, we can move toward understanding that if our situation is unfavorable due to tight cash flow, feeling bad about bills makes the situation worse, not better.

Here's something to try. The next time you get a bill, think about what services are associated with that bill. If it's something you don't need, just cancel it; there's always a phone number, and if you paid your phone bill last month, you can call it and cancel.

If it is something you use, take a minute to think about it and be grateful. When you get the electric bill, imagine the easy life you have. You just write one check, and in return, you have endless means to bring to your place light, heat, cooking, and entertainment, such as television and Wii. You can use your computer and more. All of that, and this is only electricity! Can you imagine how much you can be grateful for when the cable bill comes in? Paying rent should be no different. If you pay it in person, make sure to thank your landlord or whomever for their small part in your life—a roof over your head is nothing to scoff at.

And lastly, never ever resent any bill you have to pay, no matter what it is. Whether it is paying your ex-wife or paying a pro football player that is sitting on the DL for the season. Resentment is a huge blocker, but it's also a good indicator. It makes no difference what you resent, but be assured, every time you resent it, an order for more of it is being placed in your name. The universe knows where you live—remember, it is the one sending you the bills!

CHAPTER 18

Food

Much like money, food is also tied to our emotional lives with a thousand strings.

In the same way the subconscious uses money to regulate our financial picture, it uses our food intake to help regulate our health, physique, and appearance. There are other factors, such as exercise, stress, and other inner workings of the body. Food and drink, however, are the body's main energy source and fuel.

Before we can make any difference in our food situation, there are two facts that we must recognize:

1. *We believe that we have control over what we eat.*
2. *We don't really have any control over what we eat.*

Sure, we can decide at any given moment what to put in our mouths, plan a dinner out, or decide to eat healthy and make broccoli for lunch. But these acts are only a part of our eating picture. The real puppet master, as always, is the subconscious. No matter what we try to do, it will regulate our eating habits to match intake with the big picture: our core beliefs. Using willpower to go against the subconscious may be heroic and may have some temporary results, but long-term success is doomed from the start. The subconscious can make us eat things when we are unaware, making the game completely unfair and the outcome decided in advance. The deck is stacked, and the house always wins.

WHERE TASTE FITS IN

Taste is one aspect of eating—that feature that allows us to accept and enjoy or reject various foods based on our interpretations of their flavor and consistency. For the ego, our tastes are a point of pride and identification. The type of food we like is as much a part of us as our heritage and profession. As we have seen so far, when our egos identify with aspects of our lives—food in this case—it is a good reason to poke around and look for the hidden reason.

Liking certain types of foods can be a lot of fun and add a special quality to our lives. We can refine and expand what we like, to add uniqueness and excitement to our lives. However, identification with those things we like can be also used by the subconscious as a means to controlling our behaviors.

To understand this better, it's important to put things in perspective. Your taste in food is not a part of who you are; rather, it is a formed habit. It may point to your heritage, geographical location, or upbringing, but nonetheless, it is only a habit. A peach, for example, can be just as interesting to eat and as enjoyable as vanilla ice cream and low-fat rice milk can taste just as good as cow's milk. So why does it not? To start with, taste is almost completely objective. Of course, we will be hard pressed to find a human who prefers codfish oil over an Oreo cookie, but inside the range of the acceptable food spectrum, there are people who truly prefer things that we will not even want to try.

The best example for that phenomenon is possibly the aversion many people in the U.S. have against health food. If it has some healthy new-age word in the food's description, it just can't taste good. We had a friend over some time ago and opened a box of organic cookies. She took one look and decided that eating anything that came from a box bearing the word *organic* was going far beyond her comfort zone. These were not healthy cookies; they had sugar and chocolate and were gooey and yummy, but being organic set off an alarm for her that they wouldn't be edible. This may be funny, but it is so common. Any food titled vegan or vegetarian is also subject to odd societal stigma. A bite, maybe, but a whole meal? When you think about it, it says, "Unless there's a piece of dead animal on my plate, this meal cannot possibly be called a meal." These sentiments are so prevalent in Western society that it is astounding, especially with all the information out there about the ailments that come with regularly eating meat.

So is it that we simply *like* the taste of meat? It has to be more than that. Our subconscious minds resist even the suggestion that meat or dairy be taken off our diets. There's enough propaganda out there to support the health "benefits" of dairy and meat, and even the least sensible arguments are engraved in our psyches and are nearly impossible to reconsider. "Milk is good for our bones." Really? Dairy drains calcium from our bodies. "You need red meat for iron." Another fallacy.

Nutrition Information Has Little Impact

Our subconscious controls the point of view and the flow of information to the conscious minds so tightly that our ability to be objective and make proper nutritional choices based on sound research is almost nonexistent. We can only make choices within the confines of our core beliefs. If somewhere we believe that we are sick, weak, or overweight, and that this situation is beyond our control, information that corroborates that story is the only information that the subconscious will allow into the conscious mind. Any outside attempt to introduce a healthy lifestyle will be rebuffed. There's more than enough bad information out there wrapped in a shroud of scientific data that can be used by the subconscious to steer us in the right direction. For example, the misconception that meat is the body's choice source for protein. Did you know the average American gets far too much protein? Look in the mirror; I doubt you're looking at someone that needs more animal protein and can tolerate the saturated fat, hormones, antibiotics, and carcinogens that come with it.

Some people report that they feel that "their body needs meat." True, just as others report that their body needs a cigarette. Both needs don't prove to be what the body needs, but rather what the mind thinks you want. Your body needs meat and milk to be healthy as much as you need a pacifier to fall asleep.

TOTAL STUPIDITY

There's a lot of faulty nutritional information out there, but there are also people who see the irony and bypass it altogether. The following phrase sums up how many people excuse their poor eating habits: "Life is short, so I might as do what feels good." Wow, really? Am I the only one who sees the paradox here? If you live unhealthily, it might feel better than trying to control yourself, and that does have merit. But please know that the angel of death will not descend on you as you reach fifty-five or sixty in the form of a pretty lady, hold your hand, and lead you to heaven. The angel of death will sit next to your hospital bed as you undeservingly await a heart transplant or for the next heart attack, as your family's resources are drained. Living an unhealthy life means dying a really long, lonely, and painful death while ruining your family in the process. Eat what you like, but just know that the selfish nature of your eating habits will become crystal clear on the day you least expect it to.

LET'S GET TO THE POINT

This section is not meant to convert you to vegetarianism or even to convince you to eat healthy. If the desire to be healthy doesn't come from you, there's no point discussing it anyway. The idea is to shed some light on how food choices are made, what part of us makes them, and how.

I'm here to tell you one thing: if you are struggling to lose weight or to change your eating habits, you are trying too hard. Going in a direction that appears to be against your nature will never get you where you want to be, it will only make you feel like a failure.

Our greatest enemy right now can be our biggest ally. That is, of course, the subconscious. As long as our core beliefs are not in alignment with our desires, we will always struggle and always lose.

To refresh your memory, your desires are the wishes you make, which are known to you. These are things like, "I want to be thin and fit," "I want to be healthy," and "I want to be attractive." Your core beliefs are a large part of who you are that you are not aware of. This is the part of you that believes you'll always be the way you are, that the way you are is bad, and that you will not be happy until you do this and that.

I'm not saying that it's easy to align our core beliefs with our desires. After all, we can always tweak our desires; we can just say, "I want to be exactly who I am right now," but if that were the case, you wouldn't be that deep into this book.

Aligning desires and beliefs means shifting our beliefs. It means questioning everything and accepting yourself as you are while loving the idea of a different reality. It is not easy, and in some cases, it may be impossible to do on your own. Remember that those core beliefs are not a static entity. Core beliefs are constantly being reaffirmed by our habits, self-talk, judgments, and reactions.

Once those beliefs are melted away and replaced with more positive beliefs, true change can take place. Once that happens, being healthy will be easy because the subconscious will be on your side.

Remember, the all-powerful subconscious will take us where our beliefs point. If this is also where we want to go, then we are in the flow and life is fun, effortless, and free from struggle.

BE THERE

It's important to separate our work on changing our beliefs from the act of simply being and living life. We can't constantly work to change our beliefs, as it will be exhausting. When you do eat, procrastinate, work out, or whatever it is, be present! Let thoughts fill your head and let them go. There are no bad thoughts and good thoughts, and there are no good or bad feelings. When you do eat, enjoy every bite. When you work out, be in the moment.

The subconscious rules us by hiding our own actions from us. Being present in the moment, regardless of how painful and sobering it may be, is always an option.

CHAPTER 19

Conclusion

You must have noticed by now that most of the material you have read can be summed up in a few key words: be, let go, imagine, and allow. The framework in which those ideas float need the couple hundred pages or so worth of explanations.

The text you've just read gives an alternative way of looking at your reality, and explains that there is no reality other than the one you imagine. This idea is so simple, yet, due to our programming, can take long to implement into our everyday lives.

I urge you to read it again. Find one or two aspects that speak to you and take them for a spin. Find the tasty bits and chew on them for a while.

You did not read this book by chance. Rather, your path toward awareness and awakening brought it to you. Regardless of what you do, the material you read is making inroads into your life.

Your new path is about doing more but trying less, having more go your way while controlling less, and noticing more of the magic around you as moments of hopelessness start to vanish. Your new path is touching everyone around you. Supportive new faces will show themselves, while familiar faces may be a bit annoyed with you.

Resist nothing

Let go

Imagine

Allow

And then let go some more.

Join the discussion
Share your *life change* story
Look for *"How to Lose Your Mind in No Time"* on Facebook

Follow on twitter: @BarefootHanaan

APPENDIX I

Personal Awakening

In 1998, I got a huge project, which was creating an automation system for a stationery letterpress printer. I was going to be making a lot of money but not until the project advanced to a certain point. The president was happy to have me work on this project and boasted that he had to fire the last four consultants for incompetence. I was too naïve to understand what this meant for me. I estimated the project would take six months, and miraculously, with scope creep and delays, seven months after starting, I was set to demonstrate the nearly finished system.

Little did I know that the president got cold feet, as he did the four previous times, and hired two consultants to prove during my presentation that my system was useless. Regardless of my concise answers, he ended up throwing a fit, throwing chairs around, yelling at me that my answers were non sequiturs, and banished me from his establishment. Needless to say, I spent seven months with no pay while owning a house and having a wife, a young baby, and a five-year-old at home. Months earlier, I had quit a well-paying job so that I could be home with my family more. And so I had no source of income.

I arrived home that afternoon, and my wife met me at the door, saying, "Didn't go well, did it?" When I asked how she knew, she said that at one o'clock that afternoon the door to the bedroom had flung open, for no apparent reason. No surprise—that was the time I was being yelled at.

While this could have crushed us, it was one of the best things that ever happened to us. We realized that we missed many chances to see it coming. We decided to work as a team to analyze work situations and see what was behind different opportunities. It didn't take long before our financial situation bounced back.

We also realized that we were in a dismal social place. The people we hung around with toyed with us. We were in a position of weakness, and that had to change. We took matters to our own hands, and within weeks, like magic, we found a group of like-minded parents, most of whom we are friends with to this day.

Some years later, I was introduced to the whole connection between quantum theory, consciousness, intention, and the field and the science of living in the moment. I quickly realized that these were all concepts that I had been meddling with since childhood. From an early age, I knew that everything in the universe was connected in some way and believed that love was the driving force in the universe. When my mom suggested I read Joe Vitale's *The Attractor Factor* and right after that, Wayne Dyer's *The Power of Intention*, it was as if this path in my life was reopened, and I found that those theories had been studied and practiced all over. For the next few years, I read and listened to anything and everything on the subject. My family was sure I joined some cult and just waited for the day I would give away all my possessions and join a monastery. That didn't happen.

What did happen was that instead of leaving all that understanding on a theoretical level, I figured out ways to practice it. I had to be creative, since meditation, as I found out, was just not working out for me. I know that Dr. Dyer said it's only fifteen minutes a day, and I could force myself, but forcing anything is not what I consider a long-term strategy.

I learned how to observe my self, my ego, and my emotions. I learned to see some of my blind spots. I learned to be aware that other blind spots remained and were not meant to be seen yet. I learned to own and love every bit of my life, as uncomfortable as it became at times. I learned to let go. This was probably the most satisfying and most fun to do. One day I decided that trying was the root of failure, so I just stopped trying, almost cold turkey. My course of action was to see the future as I wanted to and then let things materialize. Materialize they did. After a couple of years, I developed an automated system that did most of my work for me, allowing me freedom to work in the yard, sculpt, spend time with my sweet family, and just relax. Since I stopped trying, my life is much better, and it wasn't really that bad before. Removing that layer of fake control from my life was like a dream. Things were happening to me and for me effortlessly. There was no struggle or anxiety, only visualization and things happening. Life was good.

Now I am writing, including the time I've spent writing and revising this book. Each time I got to the end, I realized that I have figured out so much while writing that the whole book was not a coherent piece of work, but rather a process of my understanding getting settled. I decided to stop trying to write the book. One day in July 2011, I was sitting in Wild Flour Cafe and found myself typing. I looked down, and here I was writing this book. Holy cow, I thought, I am writing the book! I was already about ten to twelve pages into it, so I figured I have been writing for a couple of days. I had the entire layout ready before I realized that it was happening. I am much happier with the result this time than with the last two times. This time, it just happened.

And so, I hope that you got something out of it. One thing. One phrase that got stuck, one piece of advice you can take with you. This is my purpose in writing it. You don't have to swallow it whole and believe everything for it to work. If one thing I wrote fits your wavelength and somehow merged with your life, then my work is done. I hope I caught you on your path of awareness and awakening.

Made in the USA
Lexington, KY
14 January 2013